The Unselfish Guide To

SELF PROMOTION

Jorge S. Olson

Published by Cube17, Inc.

Copyright © 2009 by Jorge Salvador Olson

All rights reserved, including the right of reproduction in whole or in part in any form.

Published in the United States by Cube17, Inc.

ISBN 978-0-9821425-0-9

Manufactured in the United States of America

Edited by Gloria Olson
Cover by Jorge S. Olson
Cover Editing by Francisco Javier Rodriguez
Photograph by Gustavo Mayoral

- First Edition -

www.JorgeOlson.com

Without limiting the rights under copyright reserved above, no part of this publication may be reproduced, stored in or introduced into retrieval system or transmitted, in any form or by any means (electronic, mechanical, photocopying, recording or otherwise), without the prior written permission of both the copyright owner and the above publisher of this book. The scanning, uploading, and distribution of this book via the Internet or via any other means without the permission of the publisher is illegal and punishable by law. Please purchase only authorized electronic editions and do not participate or encourage electronic piracy of copyrightable materials.

*You cannot change the world
if you are not willing to change yourself.*

Contact Jorge S. Olson

Website & Blog

www.JorgeOlson.com

Motivational Keynote Speaking

www.JorgeSpeaks.com

Contents

Introduction	13
ACT I	15
What Is Unselfish Self Promotion	15
Why Self Promotion? Why Unselfish?	17
The New Theory of Relativity	21
Finding Your High!	31
Inside-Out Promotions	43
How I learned Self Promotion	47
Be a Dream Maker	53
ACT II	59
Using Unselfish Promotions	59
Promotional Toolbox	61
Magnetic Personality	65
Caveman Promotion	71
Listen	75
Black & White	91
Big Picture Promotion	95
Teaching Your Child to Laugh	99
You Are Not Your Job	105
ABS – Always Be Selling	111
Hanging With Alpha Dogs	119
ACT III	129
Advanced Self Promotion Strategies	129
Internet Marketing	133
Your Emails Tell Stories	155
Your Image Is Everything	161
Business Presentation Cards	169
Voice Mail From Hell	175
Promotion on the Job	183
Web 2.0 & Social Networking	193
Write	203
Speaking	209
Final Thoughts	202

Introduction

This is a Must Read!

I say this is a must read because I myself often skip many book introductions to get to the good stuff. In this case the introduction is a big picture summary. It will give you the elevator pitch of the entire book in a few sentences. So don't skip it!

This book has been written in three Acts. The First Act will explain what I mean by Unselfish Self Promotion. The Second Act will illustrate how to use Unselfish Self Promotion in every segment of your life (business, personal, political, nonprofit, etc.). The Third and final Act will teach you advanced strategies on how to promote yourself using Public Relations, the Internet, and other effective techniques. This third part I consider a true Marketing Machine that will help you sell <u>yourself</u>.

Now, don't skip! You need to learn the importance of the Unselfish part of the whole equation found in Acts II and III. Without them you will not be able to apply anything in Act III. My goal after reading this book is for you to be a master at Self Promotion, or I should better say, Unselfish Self Promotion. You will use your new found powers to get a fulfilling job, be a star salesperson, an admirable family member (the go-to family member!) and surely catapult your business to the next level. You can use the concepts you learn in this book in politics, in your nonprofit projects and organizations, or to demonstrate to people how to be better individuals and strive to possibly change the world.

You will read some extremely hands-on, step-by-step, practical how-to advice and you will also read a bit of philosophical, motivational and hopefully life-changing views (I just can't help myself). After all, we are not just physical, not just emotional, or not just thinking beings, we are all of the above. To imprint who we really are on others we will have to see ourselves from the inside out, and then communicate this to others in an unselfish self promotion kind of way.

I consider this book to be also a Brand Management Guide. You are the brand manager and you are your own product. So in essence you are your own Brand Manager. What does this mean? You have to communicate to people your best selling proposition, convince others why you are so great, the finest, and the most sought after. To do this you must use Public Relations, the Internet, and candid conversation, among other tools. In this book you will learn easy as well as advanced marketing techniques to promote yourself. What's the catch? Well, you have to do it all <u>unselfishly</u>! How? You'll see, just keep reading.

ACT I

What Is Unselfish Self Promotion?

Why Self Promotion? Why Unselfish?

The unselfish guide to self promotion is a step by step strategy and roadmap to marketing yourself

You will learn the active and passive ways to catapult yourself to the front of every line and the top of every list. All of this is done by promoting, marketing, and selling yourself.

You will absolutely learn to sell, market and promote your products and company, but it's not done in the traditional, self indulgent or product specific way. It will be done the unselfish way.

First of all I must come clean and confess that I was not born a natural socialite, public relations guru or self promoter. I was never class president, captain of the football team, Prom King or the most popular kid… anywhere.

I also had to learn the concept of promotion; this is why I'm so confident you will learn it too. The only difference is that I'm presenting 37 years of observation, reading, studying, and experience in a concise, easy to learn, easy to swallow pill or book!

I will not ask you to change who you are or your social tendencies. Instead I will help you reveal who you are and help share who you are including all of your attributes, skills, ideas, experiences, and views. In revealing who you really are you will see how many people did not know certain aspects of your life and you will realize how so many more people will be interested in you. This can include your family, your boss, colleagues, customers, investors, friends, and everyone else that you might want to attract.

So why unselfish?

The unselfish guide to self promotion shows you how to promote yourself. It shows you how to be your very own Brand Manager in business, personal life, politics, or charity work.

It is unselfish because it teaches a method of promoting yourself for who you are, without being flashy, ostentatious or self indulgent. On the contrary, you will promote yourself by being unselfish.

The notion of promoting yourself by being unselfish is very powerful and you will be an expert by the time you're done reading this book.

I know you must have questions on how we'll do this. All of it will be outlined for you as we proceed.

The Unselfish Part of Self Promotion

Being unselfish is nothing new in business or politics, especially among seasoned salespeople. In sales, you place the customer first. This is an example of unselfish promotion. Unfortunately, most of the time it is not done correctly or it becomes just another overused sales phrase ranking up there with "value added" (we'll discuss this phrase in detail later).

An unselfish promoter places everybody first; family, customers, colleagues, charities, even strangers. Why? You realize that like you, everyone has needs, wants, and problems. People think about their needs, wants and problems every day, all day.

These needs, wants and problems vary depending on every person and every situation. But we all have them. We will explore these needs, wants and problems in detail in another theme. For now it's enough to know we all have them, and understanding this is half of the work, acting on it is the other half, the better half!

This is exactly why your promotion is unselfish. Because you now understand everyone in this world has dreams and aspirations, desires, needs, problems, and goals. All of these ideas and thoughts are in their mind constantly and they look for advice, solutions, help and comfort. And don't think this only relates to business or family life, it relates to all aspects of LIFE.

Everybody has a life and life transcends business, sales, politics, jobs, relationships. It is all of those things collectively, and more. Being unselfish means that you understand that other people's thoughts are more important to them than to you, after all they are their thoughts, but you still take them into account and respect them.

Now that we know everyone is more important to themselves than to others let's be the exception. Let's look at the world from the other person's view. Let's focus on their needs, wants, problems, thoughts. Let's ask people about them, their lives, dreams and needs. Ask questions and see what happens, see how people open up, accept you, love you. Why? People enjoy people that are similar to them and people also like people interested in them.

Self Promotion First Step
Understand that all people are just like you. They all have needs, wants, fears and problems. Their needs, wants and problems and how they think and feel about themselves is the most important thing in the world to them, and now they should also be important to you.

The New Theory of Relativity

Einstein has nothing on you

Don't get intimidated by the title of this chapter. I will not try to explain to you Einstein's theory of relativity. I remember Physics was a required subject in my school when I was 15 years old. It was not an easy theory to understand then, and it has not gotten any easier with the years. Einstein wanted us to know everything is relative to anything else in science; space is relative and time is relative. My New Theory of Relativity takes on Einstein's general principles and applies them to you, your life, your thoughts, feelings, insecurities and aspirations.

My New Theory of Relativity teaches us a simple lesson: everything is all relative. Our problems are relative, our success is relative, our mistakes are relative, and our feelings are relative. But relative to what, you may be asking yourself? Things are relative to everything else; relative to everyone else's problems, feelings or successes. If you have a significant problem, is it important only to you or to everyone in the planet? Does this problem matter to a war refugee or to a starving population? Or is it just significant to you? You see, it's all relative.

Many occurrences are relative to points of view, especially in dealing with problems, politics, successes, failures, even feelings. The importance of many of these positions lies in the importance you give them. It all relies in our inner self, in our power of decision making. We decide if a problem is big or small and the attention we devote to that particular problem.

Why is all this relativity important for self promotion? It is very important because we're learning the ultimate type of promotion here, not just any promotion. We're learning Unselfish Self Promotion. To understand how promotion works we need to know why people are promoting, and what their motivation for this promotion is. Is their motivation money? Is it acceptance? Is it power or fame? How about survival? We have to discover what motivates people to promote, what they promote and why they do it. We also need to put those needs and wants for promotion into a reality check, this is where my new theory of relativity comes in.

We all want to promote ourselves. We have a social instinct to survive and satisfy our necessities. To survive and satisfy our necessities we promote ourselves. We do it as children by drawing attention, using as many tactics as we can, from tantrums to comedy. And our need for attention does not diminish as we grow older and become adults, we just need to communicate it better, even if we ask for it straight out; "I need some attention."

My New Theory of Relativity places our needs and wants and our problems and sub-sequential promotion in check. It allows us to step back and see what we want to promote and why. It makes us think about our needs and wants to promote.

My New Theory of Relativity will also give us a reality check. It will force us to look at our life, our relationships, our problems, and compare them to the rest of the world population's problems. After this comparison, we can re-evaluate our life, relationships and problems and ask ourselves "How are they related to the rest of the population? Are they so dreadful? Can we fix them? Will we give them a high level of importance and attention or focus on something else, something more important?"

The Two Laws in My New Theory of Relativity

1. Our Problems are Relative to Other People's Problems
2. Our Problems are Relative to the Importance We Give Them

To Whom It May Concern

We are primarily concerned with ourselves most of the time. We prefer to think about our problems, our reality, our family, our feelings, our money, our needs and wants. Pay attention from now on to the number of times per day you think about yourself. You are hungry, you are thirsty, you are sad, you are tired, you miss someone, you need a vacation, you are unsatisfied at work, you feel sick or you feel lonely. We are very concerned with ourselves. This is part of our self preservation and it's in our wiring system. Now that you know this, and you know that you and everyone else are like this, let's take the attention away from us and place it on someone else. This is how we start developing our more sophisticated promotional skills.

By realizing what is important to us and how we think and act will give us an insight on what is important to others and how they think and act; what motivates them to act, react or do certain things. We will see the world from the other person's point of view. This is the first part of Unselfish Self Promotion.

**Unselfish Self Promotion
starts by understanding our needs and wants
and how we react to them,
then learning how others do the very same.**

The 1st New Law - Relativity In The World

A seasoned executive in New York or California could be worried about how to get that big promotion, say to a Vice President position, along with a raise or a bonus. While a young mother in Africa is worried about what to feed her two month malnourished baby to prevent yet another death.

Although very different realities, needs, wants, problems and feelings arise from these two individuals separated mostly by the luck of geography at birth, they both have something in common. Their thoughts are on their problems. And although reading the story we must think the executive's problem is not important compared to the life of a child, it is important, very important, in fact it may be the most important issue in this executive's life. You see, it's all relative!

This is a prime example of my New Theory of Relativity. We all have problems, we all have needs, and they are all incredibly important, at least to us.

It is the first lesson in my New Theory of Relativity. Our problems are relative to other people's problems. Let's put it in perspective. When you are faced with the everyday difficulties of life, when you are faced with decisions always remember the first law of my new theory.

We all know that others need us, that there are wars and starvation and suffering all around the planet, we all know some people have drug habits they can't kick, people who are alone and need attention, homeless people who are cold and need food, clothing and shelter, people who have some real immense troubles.

Once you finish reading this book and you are an Unselfish Self Promotion machine, I'm going to ask you to do some promotion for those people in need. That's all it really takes to change the world, do it one person at a time.

The 2nd New Law - It's All In Your Head

This is the story of two very different people, just like the story described above they are separated by the luck of geography. One lives in a third world country, in Mexico, the other lives in the most powerful country in the world, the USA. It is the story of how the luck of the draw placed them in different realities, realities they can't control. This is the story of two boys.

We can't control where we are born, if we are born in Africa or another part of the world which suffers malnourishment, war, or natural disasters, with not enough to eat, no clothes, no house, no running water. This can truly be called the luck of the draw, or a good beginning for both of us given the opportunity to be born in first world countries, or at least not being born into starvation. The following are two real stories of two real boys, and like all the stories in my book, they are first hand accounts. We'll see not only their experiences and their reality but we'll learn how they view them, how they feel about the cards they were dealt and why.

3rd World Luck

The first example is of a boy who was born in a third world country from a single mother, probably a common story that so many tell. He was an only son who grew up in a middle class neighborhood, but with no running water and no electricity. Since the age of nine he had to carry buckets of water from the closest water source, about 300 feet away from his house. He had to go up and down a flight of fragile stairs. Of course no running water also meant having no shower, and since he didn't have a water heater he had to heat water in buckets to bathe.

With no electricity his family used candles at night and sometimes petroleum lamps. The petroleum was sold at a store about half a mile away so the boy had to walk with two empty milk containers, fill them up and then carry them back home. TV and radio were nonexistent and they had a cooler with ice to keep some perishable food and cold drinks available. He was alone most of the time as his mother had to work fulltime to pay the bills, but he managed to stay out of trouble, for the most part.

The boy had to walk two miles to school and back every day. Mind you the roads were not paved, and during the winter months when rain poured down he had to find his way to school through the mud. He was lucky to have received a scholarship to attend a private school as his mother did not want him going to public schools.

There were absolutely no luxuries in this boy's life, only the bare essentials to survive. At first glance it seems this boy was not born happy, healthy much less wealthy.

Born With a Silver Spoon

The second boy lived a different existence. Maybe it's pure luck or just how the world works. This boy lived in the USA, he went to some of the best private schools and had the best Jesuit education. He played sports, participated in extracurricular activities, went on family vacations, his family owned his own home, the works. It's important to mention this boy had a large family support circle with everyone involved in his life, his wellbeing and his outcome.

Apparently this boy is happy, healthy and wealthy and continued like this throughout his life. But was he really born that way?

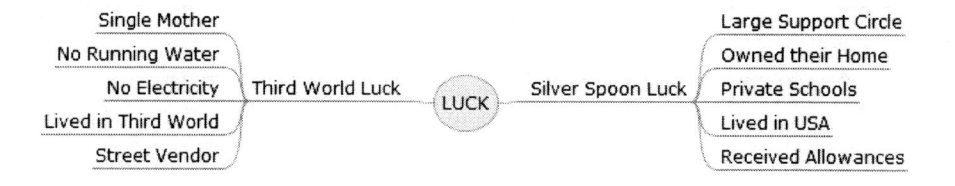

Third World Luck	LUCK	Silver Spoon Luck
Single Mother		Large Support Circle
No Running Water		Owned their Home
No Electricity		Private Schools
Lived in Third World		Lived in USA
Street Vendor		Received Allowances

So what's the catch?

I know you've only read a few pages of my book but we're barely getting to know each other. You should know that there is a catch to this story as to many of my stories. This is why the 2nd Law of my New Theory of Relativity is called "It's all in your head." You see, perception has a lot to do with reality, and it also has a lot to do with relativity. What does this mean? It means how you see the world, your life, your happiness, or the cards that were dealt to you have a lot to do with how you see yourself, how you see life, how you feel about life. You see, it's all in your head!

So what's the catch? Is there a catch to the story? Yes, the two boys are the same person. The two boys mentioned above are really me. How can that be? It's simple, just read between the lines. I live in the USA, I live in sunny San Diego, California but I was born in Mexico, a third world country. It's true I did not have electricity or running water as I was growing up and I had to carry buckets of water up to three times per day, and I have a bad back to prove it! Later on my mother managed to buy a house but we could not afford the running water or electricity or sewer system until I was out of high school. Hot water I installed only after college, and I finished paying for our mobile track house after college too.

Yes, it's also true I went to one of the best Catholic private schools in Tijuana. My mother worked hard to pay for it. Maybe that's why we could not afford electricity or running water. Later on I managed to enroll in college in San Diego. It was a two hour commute to get to school and I didn't have a car. I used public transportation to get to school and sometimes I did not have money for the ride back. I had to hitch a ride or ask for bus money. A couple of times I even slept on campus, but that's a story for another day, or another chapter.

Now you see how I got to this chapter, and to its name. First and foremost it was out of personal experience. You see, back then when I was growing up, when all of this took place, I was happy. I was always happy. Even though I did not have money, or a car, or running water, I was happy. I don't ever remember not being happy. This is why I say it's all in your head. You have to take what you have and see it as the raw materials to build something else. And always remember, you will find happiness in the building process, not when you're done building.

Find your story, your inspiration, your mission, your raw materials, your project, and promote, promote unselfishly.

Finding Your High!

With a Little Help from Others

Everyone needs to be inspired and motivated. The difficult part is staying inspired and motivated all the time, every day, the entire day, for every situation, with everyone. I call it "Finding Your High!"

Can you imagine being in a high all the time? Your high can be having positive thoughts, being content, motivated or inspired, feeling grand all the time at all times no matter what. Wow, that would be something! Athletes look for that high, that peak performance when playing their sport, businesspeople strive for it also, but we should all have it in every part of our lives. As fathers, as sons and daughters, on the job, with family and friends, while walking on the park, when working on a goal, we should all look for and find our high.

There is a trick to finding your "Ultimate State of Happiness," your high, or like I sometimes say jokingly, "Your Ultimate State of Hippieness." You have to break your life down into phases. Yes, phases, or facets. You see you have many facets in your life. Some depend on your age or where you are born, or what you are going through. Many depend on your goals or aspirations. We all have facets in our personality and in our life. We are babies, we are teenagers, we are daughters and sons, students and teachers. We are spouses, athletes, travelers, dancers, and much more. Remember, you are not your work; you are not what you are doing right now, or this year, those are just phases or facets. You are more than your facets.

You have to find your high in every facet of your personality and every phase of your life. Don't try to find your high, your inspiration as an all encompassing global form of inspiration. Break it down!

Just like you are made of many colors, you are feeling differently at different times. You need different types of inspiration at different times of your life. Sometimes you need deep life changing inspiration, sometimes you just need enough to get up from the sofa and hit the gym. Learn to see your different levels of personality, learn about yourself, about what brings you inspiration, learn how to find your high. And look for it in every facet of your personality, every phase of your life. Your inspiration may be different for every situation. Now you need to look for it.

> **Your High is a form of inspiration
> that comes from emotional experiences.**

Finding Your High is easy if you know where to look. Now you know you can look for different sources of inspiration in many different places and at different times in your life, even throughout a single day. Now your mission is to open your eyes. You have to search for that push to reach your high for everything you want to accomplish. You need to find a high to better yourself, a high to help others, a high to go to the gym, a high to find reconciliation with a loved one, to be a superstar in business, etc. Open your eyes, there is inspiration in your friends, in your family, in books, in music, in movies, in people walking on the street, there is inspiration everywhere. You just have to open your eyes, look for it, be aware of it, and don't let it pass you by. You have to be on the lookout otherwise you will not see it, hear it or even feel it.

Don't try to find a "Comprehensive All Encompassing High." Your High can be one thing one moment and then change to something else at a different time. Your High has to match what you are going through, what is important to you in that particular moment. Remember Your High has to meet your relativity! Let me illustrate what I mean with the story of how I found my "First High."

Finding My First High

I was nine years old living in my house in Tijuana, Mexico. I can still remember waking up in the middle of the night and seeing a very dim light coming from my mother's room. I was curious to see what was going on so late at night, so I got out of bed and walked towards the light. After opening a crack on her door I could see her studying at candle light with three or four candles on one side and a petroleum lamp flickering on the other side. She did not see me as I stood there outside her room for a few minutes watching her read and take notes. I did not understand exactly what she was doing or why she was up so late doing it, but I did know it had something to do with her going back to school.

When I was very young my mother left my father and as a consequence had to work fulltime to support me and send me to private school. She always enforced in my brain the importance of an education, of finishing high school and continuing on to college. She also believed in the saying "do as I do, not as I say" so she decided it was a must for her to finish high school and then college. The problem was she had no time and no money. She held a fulltime administrative job, then went to night school and the only time left to study was at midnight. I did not understand it at the time, but I did understand it when I got older and I never really forgot that image of her. It had a lasting impression on me.

When it came time for me to go to college I decided to change gears and enroll in college in the USA. After all, I lived in the border town to San Diego, California. Why not take advantage of the fact and go to school in the USA? There was a problem, though, a big one. I was a Mexican citizen living in Mexico and non California residents were required to pay outrageously high tuition rates. I didn't have the money to pay. I also only had a tourist visa to cross the international border between the USA and Mexico and soon my visa was revoked when border crossing agents learned of my intentions of studying in the USA.

Now what? I had to turn to my father. He was an American citizen from Minnesota with an entrepreneurial spirit. In his youth he ventured down to Mexico and opened several businesses, some very successful, others not so much. This is how he met and married by mother. I hadn't seen my father in years, but I managed to find him and ask him to help me acquire my American citizenship. In a matter of months I had derived American citizenship thanks to my father.

In thinking back at everything I had to go through to overcome this huge obstacle I'm amazed at how difficult everything was, but I endured. I had the persistence, drive and good will to do it and change my life. It wasn't easy and this was just the beginning. As soon as I started attending college in San Diego I realized that logistically it was a lot harder than I had anticipated.

I commuted up to three hours to get to school and sometimes more to get back home. Just to get to the border from my house was a huge odyssey. I had to walk about a mile, take one or two buses in order to get to the Mexico/US border and then decide if I would cross the border by foot and take the trolley and bus to school, about another hour, or try to hitch a ride from the border. Hitching a ride was sometimes luck sometimes skill.

I soon realized many people who attended college with me lived in Tijuana as well and crossed the border by car every morning. I noticed several cars with school parking permits hanging from the mirrors of cars waiting in line to cross to the USA. So to save some time, and some money, I started knocking on car windows to hitch a ride. I was ignored most of the time, but eventually I got a few rides. So now I had secured transportation! Not the easiest way to get to school, but it worked for me at the time.

Many times I did not have money to eat or for the bus ride home. I used books from the library when I didn't have enough money to buy my own and used the school computers for my reports. I even spent the night at school when I couldn't get a ride or didn't have bus money to go back home. I'd use the gym to shower the following day.

All through my college years, while hitching rides and sleeping on campus, I never thought what I was doing was difficult. I never thought I had a bad deal, or that I was dealt bad cards. After all, I had found my first high. Every time I felt just a little sorry for myself, or did not want to get up in the morning to start my school trek, I went back to my First High. I went back to when I was nine years old watching my mother studying at candle light in the middle of the night after working the entire day and taking care of me. My mother finished college when I was 14 years old. Do you really think I could complain? I had it easy. I was inspired.

At 9 Years Old I Found My First High!

When finding your High remember it is not just one life changing event that will influence your whole life forever. You can find small and different highs at different stages of your life and for different activities. Your High is a form of inspiration that comes from emotional experiences. You don't relive the experience to draw the high, you draw the power out of the experience and use it to push you, calm you, wake you up, keep you going, relax, or make you feel alive.

You need to find your high in every situation and phase of your life. It isn't necessarily a single encompassing high, it can be a unique high for every aspect and phase of your life, be it in sports, school, parenting, working, selling, nonprofit work, health, etc.

Illustration - Finding Your High

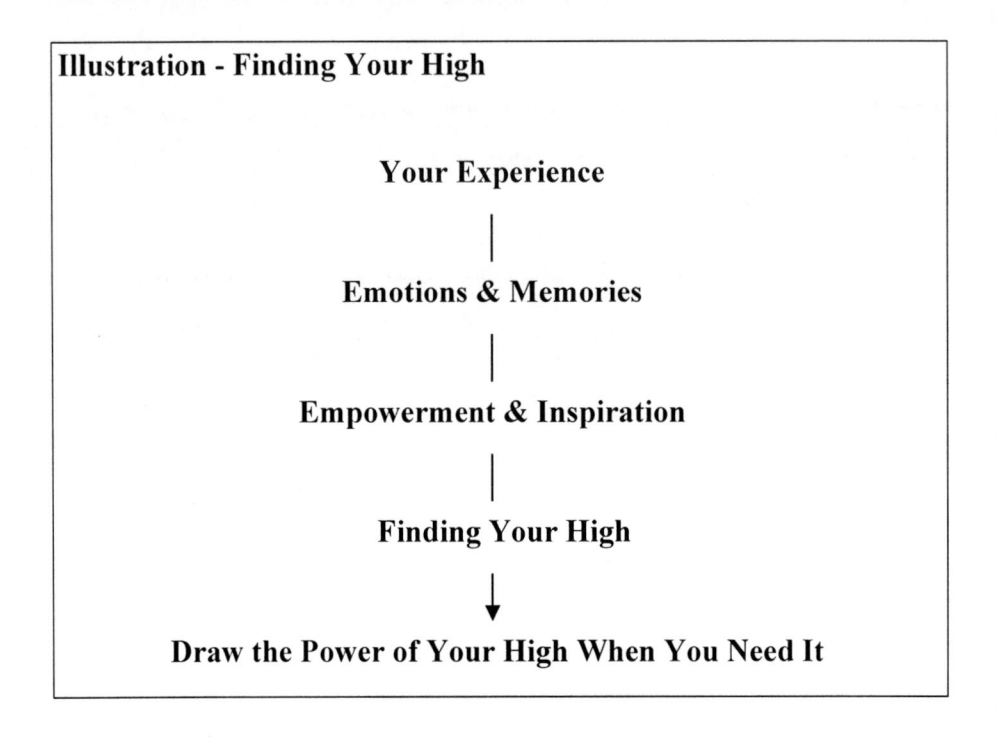

Your Experience
|
Emotions & Memories
|
Empowerment & Inspiration
|
Finding Your High
↓
Draw the Power of Your High When You Need It

Your High is useful not only to give you empowerment and inspiration when you need it, it also helps you cope with stressing situations and everyday life. This is because you're turning your experiences and the emotions produced by them into empowerment and inspiration. To achieve this empowerment and inspiration you do have to make one simple change in your thinking and philosophy towards life. You have to apply my "New Theory of Relativity" that you learned in the previous chapter. You must see the world from your point of view, from other people's point of view and compare, adjust, and learn. This way you can turn your emotions from sorrow, anger and helplessness into empowerment and inspiration. Let me illustrate this with another example.

My New Buddy

My wife and I are very lucky to be blessed with wonderful life-long friends. I could seriously write an entire book about all of them and how each in their own way has inspired us to be better people. But now I want to write about one friend in particular who allowed me to find another high in my life and, despite the fact that he's no longer with us, his spirit and life inspire and motivate me every day.

I met Christian right after I finished college. I was working as a language instructor at Berlitz, a language instruction school where he was taking English lessons. I was very intrigued by him and I asked as many questions about his life as I could. I learned he was the COO of a German software company and wanted to expand the business to the United States. Before I knew it I was on a plane to Germany to meet the owner of the company. They initially offered me a job as a consultant and I worked my way up to CEO of the USA subsidiary.

Christian and I worked together for several years. He was my mentor and best friend. He was an imposing figure, a very tall, strong and well-mannered German that practically imposed his will in business meetings just by showing up. In business he was a monster, expanding the company internationally and opening business deals and growing sales almost at will.

I had a lot of fun working for him, but I realized some people were afraid and intimidated by him. When he came into our office building you could hear his giant-like footsteps coming from a mile away. When he showed up in the office people quickly organized their desks, fixed their ties, stood up straight and acted busy. Needless to say he had a strong presence.

Christian was a life loving young man, very successful in business and probably very successful in life too. I learned a lot from him and he claimed he learned a lot from me. When I met him I still lived in Mexico and he always used to say that after a few years I imposed my "Mexican ways" on his "German ways," making him a happier, warmer, more relaxed German.

We became the best of friends and even after we both left the company we visited each other frequently and spoke frequently over the phone. He visited us in California and we visited him in Germany. We often discussed culture, friendship, and life over a bottle of wine. Every week we got on the phone and talked about our next trip to Europe or his next trip to San Diego. My wife and I relished our time together and his phone calls always put us in a good mood. He was always upbeat, making us laugh, giving us support and really making our day.

During this time I had been suffering from horrible back spasms that had lasted a few months and I could not shake my back pain, so I decided I would call Christian and among other things complain about my pain. A few weeks had passed by and I had not heard from him. I felt bad that I had not called him before, as less important things were keeping me busy. I decided to call him and when he answered the phone he sounded really tired, a bit run down and lethargic. He surprised me with the terrible news that two weeks earlier he woke up and couldn't get out of bed, he couldn't walk, he couldn't even move. He was paralyzed from the head down. By then he had received medical treatment and was a bit better and could move and walk a few steps. Can you imagine how I felt about my back pain? It's all relative, remember?

Christian stayed in bed for months and preferred that we not fly over and visit him. He lost a lot of weight and spent most of his last days at the hospital until he died. We were always in the dark about his illness because he could not explain it properly in English. My friend died at the hospital well before his time and well before his family and all of us, his friends, were ready to let him go. Christian was only 40 years old.

Christian has been physically gone from our lives for a couple of years now, but his spirit lives on in us. My wife and I frequently mention him and recall with fondness times when we were with him. A lot of things remind us of him and we are learning to use our feelings of sorrow and sadness and turn them into empowering and motivating instances.

For instance, a few months ago my wife and I were on our way to a business meeting. I had to present to a room filled with stakeholders in a new consumer product venture where I was a consultant. I did not know anyone in the meeting but they were supposed to be a very tough, cut-throat crowd. So we drove to Downtown San Diego to a fancy building, rode up the elevator and before we went in my wife asked me if I was nervous. "Nervous?" I answered. "I'm a veteran of hundreds of meetings, and besides, I have an unfair advantage because I always bring Christian to my meetings, so they don't stand a chance." We walked out of the elevator and my wife started crying, overwhelmed by a title wave of emotion she could not control.

It's true, I always bring Christian to my meetings, I think about my friend every single day, even speak to him every so often. Yes, I'm very sad about his death and I can't make the sadness go away no matter how hard I try. The one thing I can do is use my emotions and wonderful memories of him for empowerment and inspiration in my everyday life.

Inside-Out Promotions

Promote Yourself to Yourself

The very title of my book has "Self Promotion" on the cover. As you are discovering, Self Promotion is only half of the story, unselfishness is the other half, and the way you leverage one with the other will start making sense soon if not already.

In this chapter we'll talk about you, and only you. A subtle change from the last chapters, I know. The thing is, this is still a self promotion book! So why are we promoting you to yourself? Simple, although we have ourselves on our minds most of the day, with our feelings, our wants, our needs, sometimes we just do it subconsciously, we're afraid of showing that we care for ourselves to others. We're afraid of being selfish.

So let's pause for a second and forget about the unselfish part of the book and let's be a little selfish. Just a little! I don't mean selfish in a bad way, where we just think of ourselves and nobody else is important. On the contrary, our selfishness will complement our "Unselfish Self Promotion" once we manage both properly.

Confused? Don't be, the concept is simple. You have to care about yourself. You are important, what you carry inside, your passion, your feelings, your ideas, your attitude, all of these things are important. You are important to your family, you are important to your friends, you are important to the world. You have something to say, something to add, something to contribute. You are very important. And now, finally, after you master the self promotion tools you will be able to leverage your knowledge and importance. Now, before any of this happens, you have to be important to yourself. You have to believe in yourself, believe you're important; you have to sell yourself to yourself. After all, if you don't deeply, completely believe you are important and worth self promoting, nobody will believe it either.

This does not sound very unselfish does it? Well, in reality it is. You see, if you are not at your high, if you are not at your peek performance, if you are not happy and healthy, how will you help others? It is difficult to think about others and help others when you are feeling down, miserable, unhappy or sick. Whey you are down, all you think about is yourself. When you are sick you think of how to get healthier, how to take care of yourself, how to be well again. So learn to promote yourself to yourself.

Start from the beginning. You should start your self-promotion from the beginning, and the beginning starts with you. So the first idea is to truly know yourself. Clearly think about what you want from life, from your self- promotion, not just what you want now, or tomorrow, or next week. Don't just stop at figuring out what you want from work, or from your kids, or from your partner but what you want, what you really, really, want.

> **You should be the single most important person to Yourself.**

The Parent Trap

Parenting is a great example of how many people put themselves second, or third in line when it comes to happiness, attention, and life in general. Once couples have children life becomes all about the kids and less and less about themselves.

Attention to all parents out there: if you are not happy and healthy in your own life how do you expect to take care of those around you who love you? You have to teach by example how to do it! Even if you don't think your kids can sense that you're not happy or healthy you're wrong, because they do know. They might not know how to express it, they might not mention it, but they know.

Remember the quote "Do as I do not as I say?" Well apply it here. Would you like your kids to be physically, mentally and emotionally happy and healthy? Of course you do. So teach them by example how to be happy. Let them see for themselves what it takes to live a happy and satisfying life, let them see it from you.

What can you do? Think of yourself as an exact copy of what your children will be. If you have that picture in your mind you will always be on the right track. Because after all they will be a lot like you, so don't screw it up!

In order to influence others, including your children, you have to influence yourself and believe in your influence. Kids are probably the most sensitive group of people and, even if they can't explain it or completely rationalize it, they can definitely feel it. So let them know how they can be happy and healthy. Start by showing them how to do it. They'll pick it up!

Let them be confident, like you, let them know how they can be the best, like you, let them change the world, starting with themselves. Show them how to be unselfish, how to share their happiness and health so they can make others healthy and happy.

Remember that your kids look up to you. They are following every one of your steps so be wise and give them good examples. Show them with actions the right way and remember even the smallest details count.

How I learned Self Promotion

And How You Have To Take It From Here…

I did not learn unselfish self promotion all at once; I discovered it by accident and over years and years of learning and living, 37 years to be exact. I learned it in my home, with my mother and family, and later in school, in my jobs and with years of business experiences and friendships. Don't worry, I will not go over 37 years of learning year by year with you, but I will tell you how I discovered the secrets and later methodology of self promotion.

My lessons actually started with the unselfish part of self promotion. I learned most of it as a child from my mother and later on from attending a private catholic school that focused a lot of their teachings on "helping by doing." In other words, it's not enough to be a good example, go out there and do something! I did not know some of the lessons I was learning were going to convert themselves into promotion, attraction, magnetism, influence, happiness, even money. But I'm jumping ahead, let's continue with some of the lessons and you'll start putting together the puzzle and forming a big beautiful work of art soon enough.

As I child my mother often took me to orphanages. She used to collect food and clothes from family and friends and take them to orphanages that were not funded and were struggling financially. I have a lot of memories of these times and they became "part of doing business." In other words, they were as normal activities in my life as getting up in the morning and going to school. I thought taking food to orphanages was something that everyone did!

As a teenager I was very athletic and very much into sports, especially basketball, but I also performed a lot of social work through my school. My classmates and I would go to poor neighborhoods on the hills of Tijuana on the weekends and we would offer a helping hand. I remember we would cover the roofs and windows of homes; we would build water deposits where people could store clean water in their homes. We would visit the elderly who lived alone and offer to run errands for them. We registered newborns in the Municipal city offices and obtained birth certificates for them. We encountered tons of youngsters doing all kinds of drugs and we would invite them to our parish to speak with the local priests and psychologists. We talked to them and offered therapies and advice.

This social work went on for about four years, but it also prompted me to be a bit unselfish with my time. During this time I was being unselfish just for the act of being unselfish, I had no idea what was about to happen and how this would transform me into the "marketing mastermind" I am today!

> **I Did Not Invent Unselfish Self Promotion…
> I Discovered It.**

Why am I telling you these stories?

I am sharing these stories with you because I want to form a picture. I want you to follow the train of thought that I had when I discovered some of the secrets of self promotion. This way you will learn them as I learned them.

When I was 16 years old I wanted to drop out of school and dedicate my life to "charity work" or "social work." I held on to this thought for at least a few years. I was very emotional as most teens are and very passionate about everything I thought or felt. And at that time I was convinced I could touch some lives and do some good even if I had to do it one person at a time. There was only one catch; I needed permission from my mother and to my surprise I did not get it; far from it. My mother is a teacher and firm believer in finishing college before you even start thinking about anything else. So she refused to endorse my decision at the time, convincing me I was too young and didn't know yet what I really wanted out of life. She gave me a fine lecture on how I could change the world AFTER I finished college!

My mother told me I could do a lot of good one person at a time. In fact she not only told me, she showed me by example. She truly has done it all of her life. In my opinion she's even helped others one too many times. She's a true believer of giving people a second chance, even though they may not deserve it. She told me instead to focus on changing the world in hordes, many people at a time. With this strategy I would also change and help the world one person at a time. She would tell me that every little action helped, even small stuff like a good example, a smile, honest behavior, good manners, etc.

Growing up I was convinced I could do whatever I wanted in life, in society, in business, with charities, in politics. I could become the first Mexican-American president or I could be a professional athlete. I could be anything I put my mind to. I had this belief thanks to my family instilling it in me daily and also partly thanks to being exposed to unprivileged children and people as a child. I saw people struggling with their family relationships, with poverty and with drugs. After being exposed to these kinds of experiences I realized how lucky I was because I had everything; a wonderful family, an education, health, a home, everything. I was lucky; half the battle was already fought for me. And even in the rough times I always reminded myself that I was a "lucky bastard."

Lucky Bastard!

So why am I so lucky? Easy, I was born in the right place at the right time, with possibilities. I was born happy, healthy and wealthy. I know what you're thinking. Wait a minute! You grew up with no running water, no electricity, with a single mom. How is this lucky? Well, remember, it's all relative.

Yes, I was not born in a first world country but I was born very close to it, in the border town of Tijuana neighboring San Diego, California. And I made my way into a first world country sooner or later, didn't I? I definitely was not born into a wealthy family. Well it's all relative, my mother worked hard enough to send me to the best private school in town. My next door neighbors certainly didn't have that advantage. And besides, I didn't really realize I was not rich until I was about 12 years old, and I was happy all the same. This alone has given me an unfair advantage all my life because I always think that the worst thing that could happen to me financially is to be where I was at that time, with very little money, no electricity, no hot water or even running water, and even then I was incredibly happy. So I feel that advantage is almost like cheating!

You are also lucky. I don't know much about you but I know this. You are lucky because you can read, and 16% of the world's population can't. You are lucky because you have enough money to buy this book that probably costs what many people around the world make in a week (in ½ a week if you make the minimum wage in my home town in Mexico). If you did not buy it you are lucky you have good friends (and very smart friends) because they gave you the book as a gift, or because you have a library you can go to and read books. I don't know much about you, but you sure are lucky. You were born in the rich part of the world tracks!

You lucky bastard!

You are lucky. Remind yourself constantly of why you are so lucky. Do you have a loving spouse, kids, nephews, and parents? Are you a healthy individual? Do you have clothes, food and shelter? If so you are lucky, at least luckier than 50% of the entire population. You are aware of more fortunate things that you possess, think about them and think of your good memories, family and friends. You are all lucky.

Now the real question, what are you going to do with all of your luck? It's a good starting place but certainly not the goal. What will you do now? If you are not completely sure don't worry because I will provide you with a roadmap and help you make that decision. I will tell you this, though; the decision you make will surely make you a better person, and make others around you better as a consequence. This is one of the powers you will acquire while harvesting and then mastering the power of unselfish self promotion.

Be a Dream Maker

Bring Them with You

It's easy to win when it's just you. I'm not talking about you taking up tennis, or bowling, or running, or any other sport where you can compete on your own instead of in a team. What I'm talking about is we live in a reality where we can control and influence many of the things that happen to us. We can control our successes, our failures, our relationships, our future, in many respects even our health. We can definitely control our happiness. You can control whether you're "Happy, Healthy and Wealthy." This is easy; it's like playing golf. It's all on you!

Hopefully by now you have a grasp of the meaning of Unselfish Self Promotion and you are convinced that you have control over it. Later on you will learn how to use it in everyday life and after reading Act III you will leave with sophisticated tools to promote yourself to the world. This is why I had to write this chapter. You see, "with great power comes great responsibility." And after finishing this book you will start harvesting these powers and start using them for good.

So no playing golf with your new found powers. You're into team sports now! You not only have to win, but make others win as well. You need to help others be Happy, Healthy and Wealthy, not just help yourself. Again, start with yourself and move on to your immediate perimeter, your spouse, kids, parents, siblings, co-workers and expand your perimeter to your friends, extended family, group, church, neighborhood, town, city, you get the idea. Yes, you will eventually change the world!

Always expect to win! What do I mean by this? Always expect to be a winner in life, in business, in family, health, wealth, friendships. Expect it because it's easy, you control it. The difficult part is to bring people with you. Help others be happy, healthy and wealthy. Then you'll not only be a winner, you'll be a champion.

**Help others be happy, healthy and wealthy.
Then you'll be not just a winner, you'll be a champion.**

It is easy to win, to be a winner. If you don't completely agree with me right now you will after you discover the meaning and methodology of unselfish self promotion. If it's easy to be a winner why stop there, why not persist and make others winners? It will not only make others happy, it will bring you satisfaction as well.

This is why this book has the word "Unselfish" in the title. Imagine getting all this power without any of the responsibility. Well that would not be very responsible on my part, would it?

Besides, once you are completely Happy, Healthy and Wealthy, what are you going to do then? Will you just retire from Self Promotion? Will you just turn it off? Will you go off into the wilderness, build a cabin and live all alone? No, especially that last part, that's just ridiculous. It's really not; I'm trying to make a point. You will not go off and live alone, you have to live with others, you have to socialize, and hopefully you took people with you to the unselfish promotion trip and they will be like you, enjoying life, helping others, being Happy, Healthy and Wealthy in your company. Or do you want to be alone at the top of the hill, alone at the finish line, alone in your yacht?

Alone in your Yacht

Let's say you are a business person or investor and are involved in business in any way; investor, owner, executive, salesperson or highly paid employee. You make it big and you have cool toys to prove it. The fast cars, the mansions, even the boat, the great big boat. Yes you have arrived; you have one of those huge luxury yachts you used to see on "Lifestyles of The Rich and Famous" with five bedrooms and a full time crew. Yes, you have arrived. Can you see yourself? Can you see yourself sitting in the Jacuzzi sipping on your favorite drink in the middle of the ocean, enjoying the sun, the fresh air and sitting there all alone?

Everything was great until I got to the all alone part, wasn't it? That's exactly the point. It is easy to be on "Your High" but can you be high with your friends? Can you bring your friends with you? Do you want them there blissfully enjoying the company and yacht, or would you rather be all alone in your yacht?

CHAPTER NOTES:

Be a Dream Maker.

It is easy to have dreams; it's a little bit harder to make them come true.

OK, it's a lot harder to make them come true. But you know what's really hard? Making dreams come true for others. I'm not talking about giving away Ferraris; I'm talking about giving opportunities, jobs, houses, cars, a better standard of living to other people; people who are part of your circle of friends, family and even strangers. And yes, there is something in it for you.

When you place other people first they will do the same for you. It's very simple but true. Do the math. If you put just 5 people's interests ahead of yours they will put you on top of their list, this means 5 lists! Believe me, this will pay off. How do you place people's interests ahead of yours? Easy, start with your immediate circle, your family, friends and co-workers. Practice with them and later you can go broader and bigger.

Being a Dream Maker makes you an instant super success in the self promotion world. Your phone is ringing, your email inbox is full, and people want your help, your advice, and your business.

ACT II

Using Unselfish Promotions

Promotional Toolbox

Take Your Toolbox Everywhere

You are ready for the big leagues of promotion. But before we send you off into the wonderful world of unselfish self promotions we need to equip you with the right tools. In this chapter you will see an array of many different promotional tools, so many in fact that you will not be able to carry them in your pockets, your purse or your briefcase. This is why you need a toolbox; your very own toolbox filled with promotional strategies you can use in every aspect of your life. Some of the tools in your promotional toolbox will require a bit of time and work, others will be instant promotions; where you turn them on as soon as you learn them, and then use them, and then see results the very same day. Hopefully when this happens you will send me a note about your promotional experience.

Imagine you are on the job at a construction site. It's a large 20 story edifice you are building and there you are with your hard hat staring at the project, looking at the blueprints getting ready to start building. To build the whole project you have a large toolbox. It is filled with everything you need to finish any project. Now, as a promoter, you also have a toolbox, it is a promotional toolbox. In it you have everything you need to promote yourself. You have small tools, large tools, personal tools, internet tools, publicity, image management, marketing, everything.

Now it's time to go over your Promotional Toolbox. Let's list what's inside and take inventory of all your tools with an overview of how to use them. In the next few chapters we'll learn exactly how to use every tool in detail. You will see some familiar tools, some expected tools, like using public relations, the internet, etc., and others you would not expect, like using magnets, caveman promotions, and others.

In Act III you will see more sophisticated marketing and promotional tools to help you super launch yourself. Well, not just launch yourself but your company, your job, kids and family. It will all start with you. These more advanced tools will be natural progressions from the overall strategies used in this act, Act II, where you will see powerful tools you carry within you, in your person, in your life. You will learn to discover and fine-tune these tools and use them to promote yourself every minute of every day for big dividends. You will start seeing results immediately, and maybe even the same day you use them.

Below are some examples of tools in your toolbox:

Promotional Tools

- Magnets
- Listening
- Internet
- Email
- Public Relations
- Phone
- Personal Cards
- Caveman Promotions
- Black and White Promotions
- Image
- Mail
- Finding Your High
- Smile & Laughter

Magnetic Personality

Promote Yourself Using Magnets

No, I will not make you wear one of those small magnets in your ear, your neck or any part of your body. No magnetic earrings, stickers or shoes. You will use the Promotional Tool of Magnets to attract the right people, attention, and promotion to yourself.

Reader Beware! Magnets can also attract the wrong kind of attention, people, or reaction. This is the trick with magnets, they have two sides. Let's learn "Magnet Management." Magnet Management is where you learn how to turn the attraction side of your magnet, and keep the rejection side under control.

You may be asking yourself, "What does Jorge mean by magnets?" Well, magnets have the power and ability both to attract and repel. You have in your arsenal of "promotion toolbox" many types of magnets. You most likely use some of your magnets but not all magnets. You will recognize and know what they are and how they can be used "for good or evil."

Magnetic Personality – Is it a good thing?

We've all heard the expression of people having a magnetic personality. We always assume this is a good thing; that these people attract others to them. Now we will explore the Magnetic Personality Myth to see how we can use it for self promotion, and more importantly how not to use it in a negative way.

Having a magnetic personality means you are using certain tools from your Promotional Toolbox to attract or repel people. You might think you don't have control over your magnetism; that it is a personality trait some people have and others don't have. Actually it is not. Many of your magnets can be turned on and off. They can be used at different times and in different circumstances. They can be used to attract and to repel people. Do you want to attract people more often with a positive magnetic personality? It's easy, just change your magnets, use the positive magnets and don't ever use the negative ones, people will start being attracted to you.

If you are always smiling, always happy, making people laugh and making others feel comfortable inevitably people will want to be around you. You don't have to be the center of attention; you just have to be happy and try to make others happy. You have to speak with people, different kinds of people, with a happy tone of voice; you have to be comprehensive and caring. This will start turning you into a lean, mean, magnetic machine!

In contrast, we do things every day that show our negative side, our bad magnets, the ones that repel instead of attract others. Unfortunately we use many of these magnets unconsciously when we are annoyed, in a bad mood, depressed or when things don't go our way. Many times we try to hide our bad magnets and only use them at home or with our family. That does not work; our family is the center of our magnetism, the center of your promotion. If you don't completely attract your family members or your immediate circle you will not be able to go beyond that circle and attract others.

I have seen marriages end, friendships deteriorate, family relationships suffer because people choose negative magnets over positive ones. I have heard people say, "This is how I am, I can't change who I am. Take me or leave me." And you know what? More often than not people will literally leave you. Most people want to be around positive and joyful people.

Think of your magnetism as the forces of gravity in the solar system. You are the sun, bright, big, and with tremendous forces of attraction. The sun can't turn off its gravity and then turn it back on, there would be no more planets to attract, they would fly away never to return. Apply this example to your life and your self promotion. You should not change from attracting and then repelling, from negative to positive. When you are constantly being negative, criticizing others, snapping, you don't just make it better by turning on the charm once in a while. One of these days, the planets will fly away and you will be a lonely sun in the universe with nothing to attract.

Imagine you are the host of a party and you receive many more people than expected in your house. You don't know if you will have enough food, enough to drink, even enough chairs to accommodate your guests. Your spouse and other family members forgot to tell you they invited some more people. You are a little bit frustrated, maybe getting angry. What do you do? Where are your magnets? Will you snap at your spouse the minute they do something you don't like in retaliation or to show you're angry? Probably!

Well, that's the whole point of having a magnetic personality. You have complete control over it. You can choose to snap, get frustrated and worry, or you can choose to be happy, remember you are lucky, lucky enough to have a house full of people and lucky enough to be able to host a party. So feel lucky and continue using your positive magnets.

Be tougher on yourself to be better with others.

We're faced with many situations throughout our day, the week, our lives, where we need to react. We don't have time to stop and think and develop sentiments towards someone or something. We just react quickly. This reaction seems like it is a split decision, a feeling developed in the spur of the moment. It is really not. It is a reflection of how we think, how we see life and ourselves in life. If you are using good magnets and other tools constantly and consciously you will not react negatively in tough situations, you will not tolerate that from yourself. You will start seeing a shift in how you see the same situations and actually get angry with yourself if you reacted badly or if you made someone feel bad or uncomfortable. You will be tougher on yourself to be better on others.

Now that you know the different types of magnetic personalities, now that you know the ones that attract and the ones that repel, it's time for you to think of your magnets throughout the day; when you are walking, talking, or interacting with others; when you are alone in your car or at home. Think of what you do to attract people, your family, your friends, colleagues, even strangers. Think of what you do to push them away, and compensate, learn and apply the tools of attraction.

Let's go over some of these specific tools and how to use them.

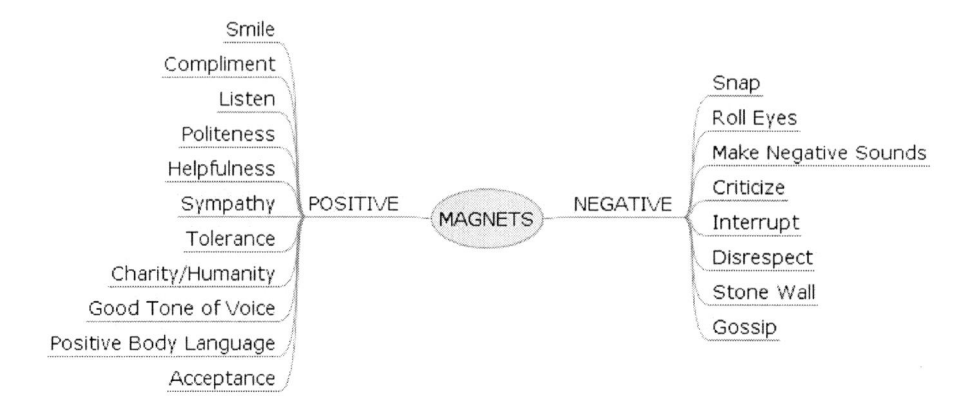

POSITIVE MAGNETS
- Smile
- Compliment
- Listen
- Politeness
- Helpfulness
- Sympathy
- Tolerance
- Charity/Humanity
- Good Tone of Voice
- Positive Body Language
- Acceptance

NEGATIVE MAGNETS
- Snap
- Roll Eyes
- Make Negative Sounds
- Criticize
- Interrupt
- Disrespect
- Stone Wall
- Gossip

Caveman Promotion

Unselfish Guide to Self <u>Survival</u>

As cavemen or cavewomen the goal of survival was simple, do anything to survive! This survival was based around breathing, food, water, sex, sleep, and homeostasis; also known as the basic physiological needs at the very bottom of the Maslow Pyramid of Needs (named after Abraham Maslow). See Figure 1. The pyramid explains how we must fulfill our basic needs before we can be concerned about superior things like philosophy, art or charity. We must fulfill basic survival needs like not getting eaten by the tiger.

The basic need to survive pushed cavemen to self promotion or in this basic need called self preservation. This was prompted by the discovery that survival becomes easier when working as a team. This includes hunting, gathering, building shelter, starting fires or protecting against predators.

```
                    /\
                   /  \
                  / Self Actualization \
                 / Pursue Talent, Creativity, Fulfillment \
                /_____\
               /            Self Esteem                   \
              /    Achievement, Mastery, Recognition       \
             /_____\
            /                Belonging                        \
           /        Friends, Family, Community                 \
          /_____\
         /                    Safety                               \
        /              Security, Shelter                            \
       /_____\
      /                   Physiological                                 \
     /                 Food, Water, Warmth                               \
    /_____\
```

Figure 1: Maslow Pyramid of Needs

Can you imagine discovering the concept of team survival for the first time? What would you do if you knew your survival depended on the survival of others; that your survival depended on the survival of your group, family, or clan; that your survival depended on working as a team? If one or more members of the team perish, get eaten by a predator or starve, you will be next, as your food and protection depends on others.

Try to imagine cavemen congregating together, working instinctively as a team, a clan, a society; going out in hunting parties five or ten men at a time. Some women are gathering roots and fruits combing the landscape while others are watching over the children and staying alert for predators. Everyone is sharing all the food, protecting each other, and realizing that self preservation is easier in groups, and if that group does not survive, you will not survive either.

> **One of the best motivators of self promotion is self preservation.**

Yes, there is a natural instinct or need to socialize and exist with others. However, it's hard to exploit this social habit, need or want when your neck is on the line. Survival is first!

In the process of survival cavemen and cavewomen need each other. It is this "need" for others that will force cavemen to make themselves and others happy, to protect others, make sure they survive, eat, drink, and be prosperous cavemen. Cavemen worry about others because others are essential to the caveman's survival.

> **Substitute the caveman and cavewoman for YOU and then substitute self preservation for self promotion.**

Like the caveman, we have to realize that others are important for our survival. Now we don't need to worry about working with others to hunt or watch out for predators, in other words, we don't need others for basic survival, especially in first world countries, but we do need others to supercharge our self promotion.

Yes, if we're alone and just worry about ourselves we'll get far with hard work and passion, but if we also worry about others and their promotion they will most likely promote us. This is true in politics, in business, in family. The lessons the cavemen learned are forgotten by many but not by you. You will always help your fellow cavemen (just don't call them cavemen). Caveman Promotion goes into the heart of Unselfish Self Promotion. It shows us a "strip down back to basics" view on this kind of self promotion and presents it to us as Self Preservation. That's a large motivation to work with others, to make others survive and prosper, to make others stay alive.

Jump ahead a few thousand years to our current reality. You don't need to hunt, to watch out for tigers or to dig up your own food. How can you use the lessons of the cavemen in your daily life, in your unselfish promotions? Try to apply the same rules as if you were a caveman, promote others with a passion, look out for them, for their interests and happiness like if your own life and happiness depended on it. Once you do this you will have mastered the core of Unselfish Self Promotion.

Listen

The Secret Weapon in Promotion

I've often heard that people who talk a lot are perceived as good salespeople. I wonder if it's because they are perceived as fast-talkers or having an ability to convince or to persuade towards a decision that could lead to a purchase.

It could be that these people are very social and enjoy talking, not only in business or sales but they enjoy talking in general. They can easily talk with friends, family, even with strangers.

It could also be that these "talkers" are visual people; they see the world in pictures, in photographs or even video. I know a few that probably see the world in high speed video. Visual people speak more, and they speak faster. One of the reasons is that they have to describe their mental pictures or videos along with all the information in that picture. Imagine describing a movie while it's being projected on the movie screen. Imagine having to describe every single screen while it's playing; every detail, the plot, the scenery behind the action, the wardrobe, everything. Well, you would probably have to talk a lot just to keep up.

Talking is not selling. Next time you observe a "fast talking salesperson" go deeper into the conversation and you will probably find out this person is visual and probably very sociable too.

I mentioned earlier you don't have to be extremely extroverted to be an excellent self promoter. You don't have to be a talker either. On the contrary, if you are a "fast talking extrovert" you will have to learn to turn all that energy into the right kind of talking, and a lot more energy into listening.

There are two very important by-products of listening: Self Promotion and Learning. Even without Self Promotion, listening is a good skill to learn and master. It starts with just listening and later in asking questions and "getting" people to talk and open up. I say open up because you don't just want superficial conversations. What's the secret to perfecting your listening skills? Now, the real secret of listening is to shut up.

My grandmother always told me "It is hard to learn with your mouth open." In other words, shut up and listen.

> **A By-product of Listening is Learning.**

Listening, and not talking, takes much practice. We are selfish by nature; we think our point of view is interesting, or important, insightful or even brilliant. Many times we want to interrupt the other person talking or "jump in" in the middle of an idea or sentence to give our opinion.

Action Items

Start to listen, deeply listen. Do not interrupt your spouse or kids, parents or family members. It is rude and more often than not it will turn off the person who is talking to you. And in the future they will not come to you when they need to talk and be heard.

Do you feel the urge to give your excuse for why something you did went wrong before they even finish telling you it was wrong? Don't! Don't assume you know what the other person is going to say.

Do you jump in with your comments while others are finishing their sentences? Don't! We all feel the urge to jump in, interrupt, and want to talk about what we think, what we do, what we feel. But try not to do this and you will see that the other person will really appreciate it and come back to you when they need to be heard in the future.

Don't make others feel like they don't know what they are talking about. Participate but not in a corrective way. Don't discredit people's ideas and points of view. Be a respectful and considerate listener.

Advanced Listening

It is important to listen deeply and relate this information to the person speaking and not to you. What do I mean? Don't try to apply everything to you, to how it affects you, to how you feel. Relate it to the speaker and to how the person is feeling and thinking. Let's call this type of listening "Advanced Listening."

Advanced Listening means you take out the SELFISHNESS from the equation. It means you are listening to learn from the other person, to offer advice, a solution, sympathy, to get to know them or to help them. Note that you don't always have to solve problems, listening sometimes means just listening!

A key element when truly listening is eye contact. There's nothing more reassuring than talking and having your listener look you directly in the eye. It shows them that they have your undivided attention and what they're saying is important to you. Don't look distracted, don't look at your watch, or your phone or at someone passing by. If you do, the person speaking may stop talking until they capture your attention again, until you look back at them again and continue listening.

Remember, you don't have to provide a solution to every conversation. This is true for personal, non business relationships. Especially for all the men reading this book! Don't try to "talk" and solve all problems when your daughter, wife, mother or sister is venting or speaking with you. Listen!! If they want your advice, input or solutions they will ask for it.

It is as important to know when and where to listen as it is how to listen. Don't try to push others to speak with you; don't try to get information out of them. There is timing to the listening equation. Don't force others to speak when you are ready to speak, if they are not ready, or they are busy, or with their mind somewhere else, they will not want to talk even if you are ready to listen.

Avoid simple mistakes like standing next to someone waiting for them to get off the phone to have an important conversation, or asking your spouse or kids to turn off the television "this instant" because you want to speak now. Wait for the right time, be patient, don't get mad or aggressive, and listen. They will know that you are listening because you are an unselfish self promoter, and already proved that you are there to help them as well as others.

In addition to timing, there is also a place to listen. Many times you are ready to listen, you want the other person to talk because you are ready, and they just don't, they are not ready, it's not good timing, or it is simply not the right place. Don't try to understand exactly why every single person has different ways of expressing themselves, or why they want to speak in some situations and they don't want in others, or even why they feel uncomfortable in certain places. Part of listening is accepting how people are, and if they are uncomfortable you have to respect it, not analyze it and try to convince them otherwise. By doing this you are doing exactly the contrary of listening and what listening is all about. Don't force people into any circumstance they don't want to be in.

Don't be a "Pushy Listener"

What does this mean? Well, I just made it up. I call a "Pushy Listener" the person that wants to know everything right now. The Pushy Listener wants to talk about it right now, they don't care if you don't. They are ready to talk so you have to talk. They do everything to make you talk; they ask you "What's wrong with now? Why don't you want to resolve this?" If you are not ready or there are too many people around they try to take you to another location, or try to convince you of why it is a good place and time to talk. They try to change your state of mind in order to make you talk. Isn't that called torture?

You can see Pushy Listeners pushing their spouse, their kids, in business pushing employees around, or salespeople pushing others to talk at this moment. Don't be a Pushy Listener. You will come across as annoying and bossy.

Remember, listening is about the other person, listening means letting the other person speak their mind, or unwind, or understand their problems, or understand how they actually want their problems solved. It is not about you. Listening should be Unselfish.

Many salespeople fall into the Pushy Listener category. Unfortunately many of them also fall into the plain pushy. Salespeople need to understand that pushing is not selling. Don't try to substitute skill, experience and knowledge by just pushing. For example, if you are a sales person, being perseverant is a great trait to have, but even better is having people call you to place orders when they are ready to buy. This type of sales person / buyer relationship is hard to achieve, so it's one that few people have. Try to establish those types of relationships.

Listening Breakers

Let's go back to your Magnet Chapter to see which magnets repel and which magnets attract. When having a conversation there are many things you can do and say to turn the other person off, to make them defensive, and to shut down their listening. The same is true when you are listening. Your posture, manner, expressions, tone of voice, eye contact, the way you ask questions or answer them, they all have to do with how the conversation is going and with your listening ability. You have to put the other person at ease, they have to be comfortable speaking with you, feel you will not get angry or snap back at them.

Put yourself in their place. If you are having an important conversation with someone and they get mad, or visibly irritated, and they are just waiting for you to finish and jump in with their point of view or to criticize you, or even worse, to make you feel bad, would you want to continue that conversation? Probably not, it's over. Don't be that person, don't prematurely end conversations. If you can't listen any longer, if you are getting angry or irritated, pause the conversation or end it for the moment. You can take a break, go do something else, and continue the conversation another day, at another time, in another place.

Talking is Not Selling

Man oh man; I could talk all day about this topic. Talking is not selling. You will see in one of my favorite chapters, ABS (Always Be Selling) that you are always selling, I don't mean that you are a salesperson, I mean you are a social being interacting with others, and in those interactions you are promoting, you are selling.

Way too many salespeople believe selling means talking or that you have to talk and talk to sell. The opposite is true, selling is more like listening. This is why now we have all those elaborate styles of selling, the most famous being "relationship selling" and my favorite "consultative selling." Consultative selling is considered the best of the best, highest of the highest, smoothest of the smoothest forms of selling. Described in other words, consultative selling is selling by listening; granted, you also have to learn to ask the precise questions.

Let Them Relate

It's hard to really get to know people when you are the one doing all the talking, and if they don't relate to you they will not like you, and if they don't like you they will not "buy" you, or buy something from you. You are always selling yourself, and in order to sell yourself you need to listen, that's your first sell. You must be a good listener.

Listening allows people to talk, to tell you what they want, what they need, how they want things done. If you don't listen you will not recognize how to successfully sell yourself because you will not know what that person or that group is looking for.

Me vs. You

Can you stop talking about you, your company and your products?

The most overlooked and understated rule in sales is the "Me vs. You" rule. What does this mean? For every time you use the words "me", "my", "I", "our" or "we" you should use at least twice as many times the words "you" or "your." For example, instead of saying "my product, my company, my idea, I do this, our price, our benefits, our points" you should be using "your benefits, your solutions, your price, you will profit, etc."

This is true for sales presentations, letters, statements, and even conversations. Pay close attention to the next email or letter you write and see if you are using these key words. If you're not, you need to practice until it becomes normal for you. Why is this important? It's not only how many times you're using a word, it shows the buyer you care about them, about their problems, their company, their solution. Why is this important? Well you tell me! Are they buying your product simply because of the product or because what it will do for them? Besides, when you are selling yourself and not a particular product you start using the right tools, the Unselfish Tools. The moment you think you're selling a product or a service you will fall into the "me" trap. You are selling yourself, not a product or service. You are selling yourself as a person who will look out for the customer in any situation, with any product. Your goal is for them to trust you completely, to call you when they need something, to have you on speed dial.

As you can imagine the "Me vs. You" rule applies to everyday life as well, not only to business. It is in our nature to promote ourselves, to see how we can place ourselves in different situations, to benefit from certain activities, businesses or social events. And it is not a bad thing; it is our "Caveman Promotion" kicking in. In Unselfish Promotion you manage these impulses, you understand that in order to succeed, to prosper, to be happy, you need others, you need people. This is why you need to make others happy, to make them Happy, Healthy and Wealthy. If you have this down, if people recognize this, you are well on your way to conquering the "Me vs. You" rule.

Consultative Listening

Business Consultants have known for many years that many of the answers to important questions and even the solutions are within a business organization, within their employees, management, suppliers and customers. Many employees within organizations don't think consultants do a great job because in their words, "consultants come in, they are given a list of problems together with the list of solutions, and then they just turn around and present them in a logical way to management." I used to work as a software consultant and some of it is like this, especially when you are dealing with business processes and best practices and with how a business runs and relates to customers and suppliers.

In this type of Consultative Listening you ask key questions to employees, managers, suppliers and customers. In essence you are listening. You have to be a great listener and ask key questions. You sit down with each individual and ask them what they do, how they do it, how they interact with colleagues, suppliers, customers and other stakeholders. You ask them about their job, their problems, what works, what does not work, and you ask for solutions. From the outside it's very basic, you get all of the answers and then you come back with the best solutions, many times the same solutions provided by the employees in the first place. Again, it looks basic and in theory it is. In practice it is not. You see, you're dealing with many people, some employees and some not, some think they will lose their job, others don't want to tell you what they do because they think if they do they will be replaced, some are afraid, others angry.

A great Consultative Listener can put you at ease, make you feel comfortable, unthreatened, like a friend. Furthermore, a Consultative Listener can take basic questions and get amazing answers. People don't always give you the best and most powerful answer the first time around. This is because they don't know what you are looking for; you probably did not ask the right questions. If you ask "What do you do in the company?" you will probably get a very general answer like "I'm an accountant" or "I'm the warehouse manager." That's not the answer you want, so you better ask different, more specific questions. You need to know the relationships this person has with others, not just what they do or the steps they take to do it.

Businesses at the end of the day are all in the people business. If you import or export, manufacture, retail, distribute, sell, buy, trade, you are in the people business. People are the best assets in a business, not the warehouse manager but the person. Find out from them not only what they do and how, learn why, learn what makes them tick, and listen.

A Consultative Listener asks deeper, advanced and smarter questions. This Unselfish Promotional Tool has two very important outcomes:

1. You will be able to ask important questions and get the correct answers, not just superficial, short answers.
2. You will place the other person at ease, they will feel comfortable with you, and hopefully they will even like you. Why will they like you? Because you care, you are not just asking superficial questions, you are asking about them, about their feelings, what they do, what their outcome is, their outlook and their options.

To better understand this Promotional Tool pretend you call someone on the phone in another part of the country, or another part of the world. Actually, pretend you call me. I live in sunny San Diego, California. Pretend you call me and you want to know how the weather is and how I like the weather. What do you ask if you truly want to know about the weather and are not just being polite? You would ask questions like these:

Consultative Questions for "How's the weather out there?"

- What's the weather like? – It is great
- *What is the temperature?* – Today it is 75 degrees Fahrenheit
- *Is this common for February?* – Yes, I love the weather out here
- Do you go out in the sun? – Yes, I love the sun
- *What do you do?* – Well, I go out
- *Do you go for a run, go to the park, go out with your family? What is your favorite thing to do in a sunny day in the middle of winter?* – I open all the windows in my house to let the sun come in and illuminate the house. I also love to go have a cup of coffee in my favorite corner Café and enjoy the sun with a book or a magazine, or write a little bit. Even if it's just for an hour.
- *Do you sit inside or outside the Café?* – I sit outside; they have a shaded patio with ceiling fans you can turn on if it gets really hot.
- *Do you go alone? Is it your quiet time?* – You got it, most of the time I go alone and get some alone time with my thoughts. It relaxes me and makes me think how lucky I am to live here.

This is a very basic example, talking about the weather. With that said, the questions took the simple, everyday question of how is the weather and got more information. What is the outcome? The obvious outcome is that with good consultative questions you get good answers. You learn more about the person, how they think, what they do, what they enjoy and how they interact with their environment. The not so obvious outcome is that you are placing this person in a great state of mind. They are happy about the sun, about where they live and how they live. You are placing them in a state of "sunny disposition," all of this with Advanced Listening.

Take the same example into your personal life. You just picked up your spouse from the airport as they arrive from a week long business trip. You want to know how they are, how they really are doing and how the trip went. Think of the questions you will ask. Is it just about the business meetings? I hope not! The trip experience depends on so many things beyond a meeting. If you truly want to know about the trip experience you ask about the flight, about the airport wait, the food, the hotel, the meetings, you ask about the weather, the people and if they were friendly. You will ask if he or she slept ok, if they had time to exercise, or read or watch TV. You will ask about the experience, the moments, the feelings. Don't expect them to tell you everything the moment they see you. Understand that they are tired and just happy to be back. This is where you turn into the Consultative Listener. Don't ask how it went and expect a spectacular, detailed story. Not all people are storytellers and even the ones who are need a little help. Ask the right questions at the right time and then truly listen.

Here is a visual of all the listening tools you have at your disposal

LISTENING TIPS
- Don't cross your arms
- Control your expressions
- Ask questions
- Don't get mad
- Be in the right place
- Don't overreact
- Wait for the perfect time
- Don't judge
- Relate to others
- Look them in the eye
- Make them feel comfortable
- Use consultative listening

Black & White

Your Grandmother is Watching

Have you ever wondered what people say about you? What people think of you? Would you like to influence people's impressions and what they think about you, who you are, what you stand for? You can, without telling them what to think and without obsessing over it. There is a simple tool in your Promotions Toolbox used exactly for this. This tool will give people not a first impression, you have other tools for this, it will give people "the impression," a lasting unchangeable impression that goes to the core of how people see you, what they think of you, how they feel about you.

It is important above all else that people know you are primarily and genuinely good. I don't mean a saint, I mean good; a good person, good son or daughter, good sibling, a good person. Many of us have different beliefs of what could constitute something good and something bad. A lot is influenced by our upbringing, by our religious beliefs or by our education. One thing is for sure, there are a lot of gray areas from just being good and just being bad, right?

This is the basis of this easy to understand but very difficult to apply promotional tool. Imagine if you would have to make decisions based on a Black and White mentality; no in-between, no gray areas. Again, this is easy to understand, and great in theory, but difficult to apply. Well, I never said this would be easy. This is the whole point. If you need a predictable, reliable, image or impression that will be stuck on peoples minds, you have to be predictable and reliable, that means making the same decisions over and over again, that means acting eloquently over and over again. It means making black and white decisions. This means applying this new tool for you and not for others. In other words, don't use the Black & White tool to judge others according to your beliefs, or to force others to make decisions according to your opinions. It means applying this unique tool to yourself, yes; you can teach it to others, I don't have a patent on it! But please don't use it to judge others.

It is very easy to say and very difficult to do. Yes, living your life in black and white is tough. After all, we are faced with many difficult situations every single day, several times per day. We have difficult situations at work, with our family and friends. Let's take a salesperson, for example, out selling, asking for the order, talking about products or services, maybe exaggerating a bit on the features or on competitors' weaknesses. Is this salesperson lying? Probably not. Is this person just expressing an opinion? Probably. Is it Black or White? Well, you have to decide that, not me. In your everyday life don't kid yourself, just make Black & White decisions. Distinguish between the good and the bad, the right and the wrong and always try to choose what's right and do your best.

Black & White Habit

Let me tell you a secret, a secret I learned when I was younger, a secret that has helped me make the right decisions, make Black & White decisions even when I'm not thinking about it. Let me tell you how to Black & White a habit.

The secret is my grandmother. You don't know her, but I'll let you use this secret anyway. My grandmother is the poster of Black & White. She taught me this tool, this secret tool, and now I'll share it with you. I grew up with my grandmother and I'm still very close to her. She's a strong 81 year old hardworking woman who had a very tough life. I could tell you many stories; probably write another book just about her. My grandmother was left homeless twice in her life with six children. She raised all of them on her own to be honest, hardworking, Black & White decision makers. Like I said, my grandmother is a very admirable woman. She always taught me with actions, words, stories and examples, including her own. She showed me how to behave and make decisions, good decisions, Black & White decisions. She always saw everyday life in Black & White and commented on it around the table over coffee and food.

So what's the Black & White secret? Easy, I try to live my life as if my grandmother is watching; whether I'm making a small decision, large decision, or any every day decision. This is how I find inspiration; this is another way I found "My High." You have to do the same. Find another high. Find inspiration in your decisions; find a way to act appropriately, to live the "right way." Find a way you can always be sure you will make the Black & White decision.

Making Black & White decisions will leave a longstanding stamp on you, your character, on people around you, your family, employees, colleagues, and everyone who knows you. This is one of the best promotional activities you can ever practice. It is not a short term promotion, it is a lifelong promotion, it is a promotional strategy so powerful it will out survive you. Your Black & White example will be here long after you are not. That's a powerful promotional tool.

Big Picture Promotion

Promotion for Life

Don't promote for today, don't promote for tomorrow, you have to promote for life.

You have to think of your promotions as a lifelong effort, an effort that is based not only on your knowledge and experience in a particular subject, not only positioning yourself as the authority in an industry. You always have to think big picture, think promotions for life.

We talked about Black & White promotions in the last chapter, a way of behavior that people will respect and a way for you to leave a long lasting mark. We also talked about Listening, a way of promoting yourself as someone who pays attention and cares about others. We also talked about promoting others and helping others be Happy, Healthy & Wealthy. All of these different promotional tools, strategies and behaviors are part of your Big Picture Promotion.

Your Big Picture Promotion is your life plan. It is your positioning statement for the next 20 to 50 years. It positions you in business, the community and politics, not just today, or tomorrow but forever. As you can see this strategy does not have a specific call to action, it does not prompt you to get a job, or to land a business deal or even launch a nonprofit organization. This is even Bigger Picture than that. This strategy goes beyond business, the community, beyond politics. It is your promotional spirit, it is promoting your character, your principles, promoting yourself.

Why Big Picture?

How will I benefit from Big Picture Promotions? What are the practical applications? These both are very good questions. Throughout life, you and many other people will have to make decisions that affect others. You also have to make recommendations, judgments, build teams and work with others. When all of these decisions are made, when you have to work with someone, hire someone, promote someone in their job, look for a partner, a political candidate, or just someone of value, when you have to look for such a person, where will you look? Who will you pick? This decision is not just left for you to make; everyone has to make these decisions throughout life. This is where the practical application of Big Picture Promotions comes in. When you apply the Unselfish Self Promotions strategies long term, your phone will be the one ringing; not just for a job or a promotion, for everything. This will not happen once, you will start seeing more and more people getting close to you, being attracted to you; it's like supercharging your promotional magnets.

Big Picture Promotion will also be reflected later on in ACT III where we go over advanced promotional strategies and real life marketing tools. These tools will teach you how to use the internet, public relations and other strategies to promote yourself and get incredible results, but remember this, without the Big Picture Promotions your new promotion is just short term, you will be able to get promotion, but for a month or two, for a year or two, or for a product or a business. After a while it will vanish and you will have to start all over again. This is why you need your Big Picture Promotion. You need to always stay on top of the promotional stack. You need to be the first person others call for any project, any party, all the time.

Yes, you will learn other specific applications for promotions. You will learn how to apply them to a job, or to get a promotion or a higher salary, you will learn how to sell products and services, or how to fund a business or grow it. There are many specific applications for your promotions and if you are now looking for a better job, looking to run for office, opening a business or just need promotion for your project it is hard to think big picture. It is difficult to think big picture because you have a necessity now. You need to sell now, you are driven, you need to promote your business, and you are fast and furious! Yes all of this is great. And like we said, you will be able to do it; to promote very specifically and successfully, but you will have other projects, other businesses, other situations, so when you can think big picture, and think for life.

> **Promote for Life,**
> **not for a job, not for a project, not just for a business.**

Teaching Your Child to Laugh

ABS – Always Be Smiling

Your smile is a promotional tool you use everywhere, everyday, all the time. It is almost a permanent tool that must be part of your promotional toolbox. You can't shake it, you can't take it off, and it's always there. The good thing is it is not just for show, not just for promotion. Smiling and laughing will also promote you from the inside. It will help you be happy and healthy. Wearing a smile should be part of you, part of your image, your personality, your character, but it also reflects how you see yourself, your life, the world, and situations around you. Laughter is a magnet, it attracts people to you, it makes people wonder why you are happy, what you know, what you are smiling about. There is a certain mystery about a person who is always smiling.

Laughter is a natural, instinct impulse, but it can also be taught. Imagine making it a point to teach every child to smile; your kids, grandkids, nephews, nieces, all kids. It is important to teach your kids to laugh, teach them as babies to laugh loud and often. As they grow older continue to make it a point to laugh with them and show them how if they forget or choose not to laugh.

Big Surprise – It's not all laughs

I was really surprised to learn it's not all laughs. People started to ask me only a few years back why I was smiling all the time. Others noticed that every member of my family was also always smiling, even laughing out loud in times of happiness and even trying to do it in times of sorrow. I must admit these comments were a surprise to me. I thought laughing and smiling was normal for every family until I sadly discovered it wasn't. This is why I decided to write about it.

In my clan all the adults and even the kids teach babies to smile. They are constantly making them laugh and I never thought anything of it. I thought this happened all over the world in every single family. I see it doesn't happen, but it must. Smiling is one of the most magnetic tools you have in your toolbox. It attracts people to you, makes them wonder why you are happy, or if you are always happy, it makes people feel good and at ease.

I've always tried to have a smile on my face. I'm happy most of the time. Yes, people comment on it, especially friends and family. My wife finds it amusing that I always wake up with a big smile on my face. She likes it and now she tries to do the same. I never thought it was such a powerful promotion tool.

I attend many trade shows throughout the year, but I specifically remember one I attended where I was representing one of my businesses and selling products to supermarkets. I remember, like I do in every show, approaching people passing by, starting a conversation, answering their questions, and offering samples and brochures of our products. It was no different from other trade shows I'd attended. Some of the booth visitors noticed that I was smiling and asked me if I was happy. I told them that indeed I was happy (despite my back pain and hours and hours of standing in a confined space). They told me "You look happy, you're energetic and always smiling." I thought nothing of it; it was not the first time people asked me if I was happy. An hour later out of the blue someone else asked me "Why are you smiling?" I answered "because I'm happy." They laughed and continued on their way. Later on these same people came back with one of their colleagues, a buyer at a large, well-known company. They told him "Here is the happy guy I told you about." They did not tell him about my company or my products, instead they mentioned that I was the happy guy, simply because I was smiling. In the back of my head I made a mental note. I realized people do notice, I started wondering if people were telling me about it, how many were not saying anything, just thinking about it. I started being conscientious about smiling and looked for people's comments and reactions. I wanted to see if it was just my imagination or if smiling was as powerful a tool as I thought it was.

I was surprised when person after person commented to me about why I was smiling all the time; in meetings, at social gatherings, even in the cold, long meetings in board rooms. Something else happened, I started to notice not all people smiled; for sure they did not smile all the time, not even a little bit. This was actually a big shocker to me. I asked myself "Why are they not smiling? Are they not happy or do they just don't want to show they're happy?" The more I saw people not smiling the more I thought that they were in pain, stressed or depressed. Why don't they smile? Aren't they Happy, Healthy and Wealthy? Remember, ABS – Always Be Smiling!!

I decided to add "Smiling & Laughter" to your promotional toolbox after a doctor's visit. Yes, I've talked about smiling before; I even wrote a short story about it called "Teaching Your Child to Laugh" like the title of this chapter. Although it has been in my mind as something you need to do to be in a happy state of mind, I never imagined I would include it in this promotional book. That is until that doctor's appointment I had earlier this year.

I went to the doctor for a checkup appointment I had. I was in a lot of back pain and I needed to get it checked out. My wife decided to go with me and drive me there, and as we were leaving my house my mother was coming to visit. I told her where we were headed and she decided to tag along. (No, I don't usually take my mom to my doctors' appointments, it was a coincidence). Once there the nurse came out to the waiting room and called my name. I stood up with a big smile on my face. She took my blood pressure and other vitals before sending me to see the doctor. As I was leaving I stopped at her nurse station to thank her with a smile and she told me "You came in with a smile and now you're leaving with a smile, we don't see many people smiling when they come to the doctor. Thank you for smiling! Your mother did a great job teaching you to smile. Tell her for me the next time you see her." I did not know this nurse. I had never seen her in my life, but she made a point. So I said to her "You can tell her yourself, she's outside in the waiting room." And she did. The nurse came out to the waiting room and thanked my mother. WOW, I thought, I need to write about this story and share it with others. Never underestimate the power of a smile. It will always affect you and others in a positive way.

You Are Not Your Job

What Do You Want To Be When You Grow Up?

One of the "Promotion Traps" that we all fall into is promoting ourselves depending on what we're doing at that particular moment; depending on our current job or occupation. We might see ourselves as a salesperson for a particular company or of a particular product. Maybe we see ourselves as the executive at a firm, or as a lawyer, a musician, artist, or soccer mom. The truth is that we are much more complicated than that, we could be multiple things at different times, even multiple things at the same time.

Imagine yourself being in conversation at a cocktail party, talking with many people, and as with many conversations, people ask you "What do you do?" This is a significant question and asked in many different ways it could mean "Where do you work? What do you do for a living? What type of business do you have?" These are all important questions, but usually all with a catch. Why do I say with a catch? Because your answer could be limiting, limiting to you, to them and especially to your promotions. You don't want people thinking about you and just saying "That's Bob, he sells insurance, or Mike is a lawyer or a writer." You are much more than that, you can contribute to their business, any business with fresh new ideas if they would ask you. You could be an investor, a philosopher or a dancer all in one.

So what do you say when people ask you about what you do? Well, this is the perfect time to practice your promotion and leave a lasting impression on the other person. Now be careful, don't tell them just your occupation, or just your hobby, tell them who you are, not what you do. Be specific and tell them you're a lover, a visionary and a poet! Don't tell them you're a warehouse manager, that's not who you are.

This is the perfect opportunity to put your new found Unselfish Self Promotional knowledge to work. It's where you open your ears and stop talking and start listening. You see, when people ask you about what you do you should ask them what they do. Don't even wait for people to ask you, remember it's not about you, it's about them. Very few times I've been asked first what I do. I'm always sincerely interested in what other people do, how they do it, who they are (not just what they do for a living). I ask questions, pressing questions, and I try to learn. If I have some advice, a book to recommend, an entertaining story or some way they can improve their hobby, business or passion, then I start talking. I start talking when I have something of value to offer them and in most cases, after I offer sincere helpful information, they turn to me and attentively ask "What do you do?" Then I can throw in a bit of self promotion, "One of the things I do is…." Then I talk about marketing, writing, consulting, entrepreneurship or some other business related attribute.

Now, this does not always happen in business or in cocktail parties. The same applies to everyday life, buying a car, handling problems with kids or family members, and other everyday events. Remember you are not just promoting your business attributes, you are promoting yourself.

Jumping Ship

I get a lot of sales calls related to different businesses I have. Everyone gets these sales calls. People sell you food, insurance, gas, supplies, cars, telephone long distance, cell phones, clothing in a store, you name it. Many times I get to know salespeople that call me not to sell me personal use products or services but businesses; things like supplies, merchandise, services and more. I've been involved in the beverage industry for a few years now and have many people calling me for advice, business opportunities, consulting and joint ventures. Everyone who calls is convinced that they have the best looking, or best tasting product in the world, they tell me their product will sell incredibly, that people love it, and they read me all the beverage attributes.

I've been around the block a few times so I can see through most of the products, the people behind the products or the business plan to know how the product will fare in the marketplace. But what really strikes my attention is when these same salespeople jump ship and go to another company, start another beverage or even another product they think I can help them with. They call me with exactly the same pitch, the same story, different product. "This product is much better that the other one, this product is great, it is the best looking, it is the best tasting." I always tell them the same thing, "I bet on the jockey not on the horse." Meaning it is not necessarily the product I focus on, it is more the people behind it, the manager, the owner or entrepreneur. Sell yourself, not your product, sell yourself, not your business. You might have different products, different businesses, different goals, projects and passions. Yes, for sure, promote them, but promote yourself before anything else.

> **Promote yourself, not your job, not your hobby, not your business. Promote yourself.**
> **You have much more to offer than your occupation.**

What will you be when you grow up?

Hopefully you are a kid at heart, if not, strive for it! As a kid, you can be different things at different times and at different ages. Maybe Superman or Wonder Woman crossed your mind when you were a kid, maybe a fireman or a princess. We tell kids they can be anything they want to if they really put their mind into it. How about us kids, the kids at heart? What will we be when we grow up? Personally I don't know yet. Why would I want to grow up? Let's tell our kids they can be anything and they can be everything. After all they will not be a job or an occupation. Let's teach children and, in the process, ourselves to be everything.

Think of your dreams, of what's fun, of your hobbies, your aspirations and your dreams. We might have different thoughts at different times in our lives and that's perfectly fine. We need to go through experiences and stages, learn from those experiences and go to the next dream, next stage or next experience. Go ahead, be an entrepreneur, be a poet, then a painter; you can then change to a dancer or teacher. Why not? Ask yourself what you dream of being? Everything and anything!

Start by making a crazy list, a crazy list of what you want to do when you grow up, really, write it down. Don't break it down by age or category, just write it down. Don't write superficial things like a super fast car or a plane, instead write down experiences like being a pilot or a race car driver.

Let me share with you my "Grown up List" of things I want to be when I grow up. I've added experiences that I want to live and I also included some I already lived and liked, or musts I have to live. Please, no laughing. My list started when I was around 9 years old.

See my "Grown up List" on the next page…

WHAT I DREAM TO BE WHEN I GROW UP

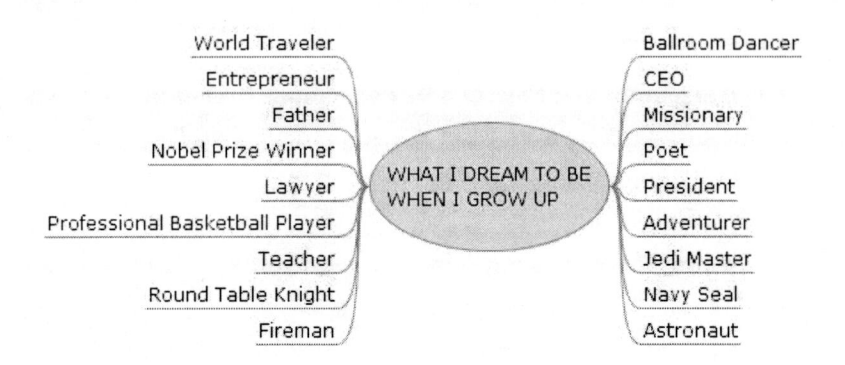

- World Traveler
- Entrepreneur
- Father
- Nobel Prize Winner
- Lawyer
- Professional Basketball Player
- Teacher
- Round Table Knight
- Fireman
- Ballroom Dancer
- CEO
- Missionary
- Poet
- President
- Adventurer
- Jedi Master
- Navy Seal
- Astronaut

ABS
-Always Be Selling-

You Are Always On...

When I was in college struggling to choose my major I never said to myself "I'm going to be in sales when I graduate." Actually that was the furthest thing from my mind. I never wanted to sell anything nor did I intend to be a salesperson. I always pictured in my mind a used car salesperson hounding and pushing people around to get the sale. I said to myself, "I'm not doing that."

Slowly I realized that many social interactions, not just commercial interactions, require sales; in normal conversations, in social gatherings, convincing your kids or spouse to do something, and many other normal social activities require some kind of convincing, or getting your point across. When I looked at it in this way I started to change my mind a bit concerning the activity of selling. I started looking at selling differently. I saw that we are always selling. When we are making a point we use sales skills, as children when we want a toy we need to convince our parents and use many tools from begging to crying to logic. As students if we need a grade changed in a report or exam we need to sell our point to the teacher. Or if we need to get into a full class we have to sell ourselves into the class. In many situations, in daily life, we're always selling.

Later I found out in the job place and in "grown up life" everything is related to selling. To write a resume is to write a sales letter, an interview is a sales meeting, getting a raise is an up-sell, getting a promotion is a long sales cycle; and that's in any job, not a sales job. Wow, and I thought I would never have to sell anything. I was surprised.

I started studying sales and applying sales to all kinds of life events, I especially applied many sales strategies to my job. For example: When I discovered that getting a raise was just an up-sell, and that to close a deal you need to "ask for the order" and that to close a deal it could take six sales calls, I started asking for a raise every couple of months. When I got a "no" I just asked again, and again, and changed my strategy and asked again. When I finally got a raise I asked for another one in 3 months. Then I asked for a promotion. If I got a "no" I asked what I needed to do to get the promotion, I did it and asked for it again. This was my first job out of college and I did not know any better. The result was getting my first CEO position at age 28 for an ERP software company. I thought to myself ABS –Always Be Selling!

> **Four basic points when selling:**
> 1. **Observation**
> 2. **Listening**
> 3. **Making others happy**
> 4. **Solving problems**

Perceive selling as a new kind of word, it's not a bad word; it's actually a good one. Sales strategies are based on observation, on listening, making people happy and on solving problems. These four basic points are a wonderful base for unselfish self promotions. You can't go wrong in self promotion when you are making people happy and solving their problems, and that's what selling is all about. A good salesperson is the one that can achieve these two last points. So be a good salesperson and start making more people happy and solving more of their problems.

ABS (Always Be Selling) means you are always at your best, you are always smiling, you are always watching out for other people's needs and wants. You behave in the best manner, you don't use foul language, you upkeep your image, and you are your best brand manager.

Remember you are always selling, you are always on. I've always noticed waiters at restaurants how they behave in and out of the retail floor. You see, for waiters the kitchen is next to the restaurant floor. The waiter stations are on the floor. Waiters are usually very professional, friendly and well behaved, especially in high end expensive restaurants where they can make great tips. I pick this example because you can observe sales behavior for yourself very closely, study it and see if the waiters and waitresses are always on. What I've noticed is they are usually not always on. Yes, when they are directly in front of you they are on. When they speak with you they are on. When they collect your money at the cash register they are on. They greet you; they are polite, well mannered, and friendly and provide good service. Now, observe them when they go to their station or to the kitchen, or behind the counter with other employees. Listen to them, many times you will hear foul language, many will talk loudly, count their tips, make loud jokes or make fun of customers. Next time you are in a restaurant pay close attention. Please don't do it to criticize or complain, do it to learn, to learn what it takes to be on, always on, what it takes to ABS.

Discovering Sales

I did not know that we are always selling. Like many of the points, tools, and strategies in this book I discovered it through my life experiences. Even though I now see every job or business as a "sales position" I did not always see it this way in the past. Like I said before, I never wanted to sell anything. I wanted to go the other way, completely away from selling. One day, I was about 20 years old, a friend of mine asked me to work at a men's clothing retail store as a clerk during the Christmas season. I needed the money and could not get any of the jobs that I wanted so I took it. It turns out that being a clerk in a retail store means you are a salesperson. Oh no!

So there I was, a new kid amongst old pros. My colleagues were all professional retail salespeople, some of them with 20 years experience. I saw how they worked, how they interacted with customers, how they approached them and how they sold. I did not like it! Yes, they were well trained and had a lot of experience and sold very well, but I still did not like their methods. They were not selling themselves, they were not solving a problem or fulfilling a want, they were out to sell. After a while of observation I decided to place myself in the customer's shoes. When I go into a store I don't like people following me around the store standing behind me. I don't like it when they ask if they may help me, I just don't like it! So I ignored my retail sales training, I ignored my colleagues coaching and I followed my gut, my Unselfish Promotion gut feeling. When customers came in as a rule you had to approach them and speak with them. This is company policy in many stores, it helps with customer service, reduces stolen goods, etc. Yes, I still approached and spoke with people but not to sell them anything. I decided I would provide information. So I told them where the deals were and when we would have discounts. I told them what to stay away from and if another store had specials. My boss did not like my approach. She told me I was not selling; I was sending people to the back of the store to buy from the discounted rack, or to other stores to buy from the competition. Yes, I told my boss, I would love it if someone would do that with me.

Imagine walking into a store and the salesperson tells you how it is, that their clothes is overpriced and they can find something cheaper down the street, that in the back of the store you find the best deals and that you should not buy the items in the front because they will be marked down next week. Wow, I would love that, unfortunately nobody has ever helped me in this way, so I decided to be the first! I placed myself in the customers' shoes. Looking out for them, helping them understand who they are and why they are shopping, and their budget. I spent most of the time asking questions and listening to customers, my boss thought these were all my friends coming in to say hello and not real customers because I spent so much time conversing with them. In reality they were customers.

The result? Well, you can imagine it. I was number one in sales in 9 out of 10 categories outselling the old pros. What was the one category that I did not win? Items sold per transaction. When someone bought one item I did not up sell them to another if they did not need it. So I lost that category!

This is when I discovered selling was not so bad. I never thought I was selling, I even ignored my sales goals and just tried to focus on making people happy and solving their problems. It turns out that in the process I made friends and had a good time. I did not make a lot of money in that job, I was making minimum wage with no commissions. The knowledge I gained was invaluable though, aside from making very good friends and having terrific experiences I discovered the principles of ABS – Always Be Selling. You see, when you are working in a retail store you have to be happy, smiling, charming, looking great, well groomed, on your best behavior, you always have to be on, you have to always be selling.

This example is not only for a sales position; it is not aimed just at making you a better retail salesperson. It is making a point, the point that the traditional use of the word sales does not apply in Unselfish Self Promotion. The new meaning of sales is that you are always on.

You are on your best; you are solving problems, representing yourself in the best way possible. You have to pass all of the socioeconomic barriers first, the first impression, second impression and third impression to get to the real you. We will cover more about first impressions and how people see you when we get to advanced strategies and when we get to your image. For now, be in your best behavior, look your best, feel like a million bucks, make people happy, solve their problems and Always Be Selling.

CHAPTER NOTES:

"You can't teach others how to sell." This is a theory I hear time and time again. "You have to be born a salesperson; you can't teach it." "Either you have it or you don't." "Selling is an art." Well, nonsense. Selling is a science. You can experiment with it, apply the same rules and come up with the same results. There is not ONE style of sales; there is not ONE type of salesperson or personality. You don't have to be fast talking, extroverted or even "smooth." Salespeople can be quite introverted and even rough around the edges.

Everyone is a salesperson.

You might think you are not a salesperson, and you might be right. Most likely you are wrong (sorry). You probably sell almost every day of your life without even knowing it. You have sold if: you have asked for a job or been in a job interview, you have asked someone on a date, convinced your kids to do something or convinced your parents you needed to do something, asked for a raise, for a discount on a car or other purchase. Many decisions in life are sales decisions. In many of these you either sell or are sold to. If you did not get a raise your boss sold you. If your kids did not do what you wanted they sold you. If you got that discount that you wanted on a car you sold them... Well, now that we've established that everyone is a salesperson and that you have one sales situation after another, don't you think you should at least know a bit about selling? How to get that job, that discount, convince your kids or even your wife or husband?

You are always on.

Remember you are always on, you are always working, selling, promoting, helping. When you are out, at parties, traveling, always be on, always look at your image, have business cards, behave, be on...

Always be needy!!

Why do I say this, always be needy? What I mean is that you have to awaken the mind's caveman survival mode and keep it on at all times. This is the NEED to survive. Survive when you need to climb a mountain, when you have to run away from the tiger that's chasing you, when you lose your job. Always be needy, always be on!

Hanging With Alpha Dogs

Alpha Dogs will show you one of the best self promotion strategies of all time!

Alpha Dogs are the people that just happen to know a lot of people and are popular, recognized and respected by others. They are those people you know that might know hundreds of people. Whether it's in their nature to be sociable, or their family is well known, or they have some connections, they are known in their job or charity organization. Imagine having not only one Alpha Dog in your rolodex but two, three or twenty. You automatically have access to hundreds even thousands of people.

Alpha Dogs are not necessarily winning a popularity contest or aren't the typical high school football captain or homecoming queen. Alpha Dogs come in every shape and size. They could have become alpha dogs in politics, they might be published writers, or have a popular blog or website read by many or subscribed too by many. Alpha Dogs can also be good Unselfish Self Promoters that help others and are sought after by many. You might already know many Alpha's without even knowing it. They could be your friends or friends of your friends.

Finding and getting to know Alpha Dogs is easy. Even becoming an Alpha yourself is easy. Learning to work with them and access their network is a different story, though. It may not come as easy. After all, you can't just walk in and ask them to call all of their friends every time you have a project, product or event. Always remember, you are promoting yourself, not a project or a product, but you. This is the approach you will have to your promotion and it will not change when you're promoting with your Alpha's. You have to help them promote themselves, be unselfish, and in turn they will promote you to their friends, family, and their whole network.

It does not matter if you're involved in a nonprofit function, promoting a product or looking for investment for your company. Alpha Dogs are the best of the best for getting the word out. The key here is how you work with them, approach them, and get them on your side. I remember one time one of my friends who happens to be a super Alpha bought a new watch and wore it everywhere. The watch was not a very expensive watch but he loved it and it looked great. He told all his friends about the watch and, you guessed it, soon after, several of his friends bought the watch from the same person he did. When he told me this I thought to myself, wow, what a wonderful Alpha Dog story about promoting not just a brand but a retailer. The irony is nobody asked him to promote it, nobody paid him, and he did it because he believed in the product. This is just one very small example of how Alpha's can help with your promotion.

When you think about Alpha's you have to think small and you also have to think big. You see, a few Alphas in your immediate circle can charge your promotion efforts quickly and effectively. A few high profile Alphas like actors, athletes and politicians can supercharge your efforts. This is the reason companies pay them to wear their products and promote them in the media. Their circle of influence can go around the world.

About Alpha Dogs

We often look to nature to meditate, concentrate, admire, and to learn. In this chapter I'll use the nature analogy of Alpha Dogs. We'll see what alpha dogs are and how we can learn from their behavior and leverage the Alpha Dog to be one of the best self promotional strategies of all time.

I was sitting back at home watching one of my favorite shows called the Dog Whisperer, hosted by Cesar Millan. The television show is about a Dog Behavior expert that travels to homes and fixes dog behavior problems like excess barking, biting, chewing your favorite shoes, etc. Although I grew up with dogs I don't have one now and I don't really watch the show to learn about dogs, I watch it to learn about people. You see, most of the time the problem is not with the dog, it's with the dog owner. So the Dog Whisperer, Cesar, goes to dog owners' homes and discusses with the owners their dog problems and concerns. He then takes about ten minutes to fix the problem with the dog and the rest of the program he focuses on fixing the problem with the owners.

Why is the dog problem usually with the dog owner? Well, most of the time the owner does not know anything about how dogs behave naturally, how they behave in the wild with other dogs. They think dogs are meant to be with people and that dogs know how to socialize with people. The opposite is true, it is people that need to learn how to socialize and interact with dogs, and after all, we're supposed to be the smart ones.

In the show Cesar explains to people that dogs are very sociable animals accustomed to live, socialize, and travel in packs with other dogs. Their social circles are large and organized. Yes, there is one dog in particular that usually heads the pack, known as the Alpha Dog. This Alpha Dog is the leader and everyone else follows. In the television show most of the time the dog thinks it is the leader of the house, or the Alpha Dog, and it acts accordingly. The dog does as it pleases, barking, sometimes biting or behaving badly. In reality the dog is not behaving badly, the dog is behaving like a dog. The human needs to learn how dogs behave and turn themselves into the Alpha Dog of the family. As soon as this is achieved and the dog understands he's not the Alpha Dog anymore the problems immediately end. This is why I always say that Cesar Millan, the Dog Whisperer, should be Cesar Millan, the People Whisperer. In my opinion more than a dog behavior expert he's a human behavior expert.

The analogy in this chapter "Hanging with Alpha Dogs" teaches us how to take that example from nature and apply it to promotions. You must see how dogs follow their pack leader, take their example, walk when the leader walks, behave like it behaves. In promotions we should look to the human equivalent of the Alpha Dog; the person who not only knows a lot about people but is respected, admired, and seen as an example by others.

Alpha Dog Matrix

In our following example you will see how having access to one typical Alpha Dog can introduce you to 240 people that they have direct access to. The Diagram Alpha 1 illustrates how an alpha dog might know different groups of people. One group could be friends from school, another could be acquaintances at a sporting club, or they might belong to a social club, or other association where other people gather. Don't think Alphas just have one big group of people they know and gather with all the time. More likely they have different groups with different people. In the diagram Alpha 1 you see just the first part of what could be a much larger matrix. In our example you see the direct connections only, in other words, people your Alpha Dog knows directly. Each one of those 240 people knows at least 100 people and has at least 10 people in their immediate circle of influence. This means your promotion can reach out to 2,400 people under this example with Alpha Dogs. Get a couple of them on your side to promote and you can easily reach 10,000 people.

This graph shows an example of a matrix of Alpha Dogs, where you can have access to a few Alphas and expand your promotional reach to hundreds or thousands of people quickly.

This type of matrix can be very powerful. There are other considerations to the matrix that you have to learn before you approach it or want to promote through it. You see, not all matrixes are made of the same receptors or people, the people in the matrix have different interests, are of different ages, and different economic backgrounds. If you are looking for a matrix of students you would not approach your parents or grandparents and start looking for Alpha Dogs through them. You would contact young people, other students, maybe class presidents, tutors, teachers, student associations, fraternities, sororities, clubs, athletic departments and so on.

The Unselfish Guide to Self Promotion

Diagram Alpha 1 – Alpha Dog Matrix

Try to use Alpha Matrixes to promote yourself using Unselfish Self Promotion. Don't try to immediately push your products or services through your Alpha Dog contacts, you will fail, and most importantly, you will burn a very powerful matrix of as much as 2,400 people. If you push your company, product or service from the get-go they will not see you as unselfish, just as a promoter. Don't be seen as the "email spam" of promotions.

Alpha Matrixes can be used very effectively to promote yourself and later on to promote your projects. Like in all promotions, you have to be very creative and follow through with your promotions. For example, if you want to promote a specific project, cause or product you could print t-shirts about your project. You then have to find Alpha Dogs to wear the t-shirts, talk about them, talk about the project and set the matrix on fire. The best and most recent example I can think of is (PRODUCT) ^{RED}, a project created by Bono and Bobby Shriver to raise awareness and money for The Global Fund by teaming up with the world's most iconic brands to produce (PRODUCT) ^{RED} branded products.

It is an Alpha Dog Matrix put together like few can. Bono is the Alpha promoting the "Red" products that started with t-shirts, cell phones, credit cards, iPods, and laptops. You buy these items at participating retailers and a percentage of each (PRODUCT) ^{RED} product sold is given to The Global Fund. The money helps women and children affected by HIV/AIDS in Africa.

Can you imagine the matrix Bono created? Can you imagine the other Alpha Dogs Bono just happens to know or can reach? I've seen numerous stars like Julia Roberts, Penelope Cruz and Natasha

Bedingfield promoting the Red project. I've also seen Oprah promoting it on her TV show. Countless other rock stars, movie stars and athletes are behind it. Now that's something.

Bono's Alpha Matrix, as you can imagine, is not to sell t-shirts or cell phones. It goes deeper than that. His goal is designed to help eliminate AIDS in Africa. This wonderful project started an educational movement teaching us that we can do something to help. When asked by Larry King why he got involved in this project Bono answered "Someone needs to do something about it." That someone just happens to be him. And actually he's extending the invitation to everyone in the developed world to participate in this change. And the time is NOW.

The movement involves simple actions like buying consumer products such as T-Shirts, phones, shoes, hats and many other products. He's proving that anyone can make a difference. Just by buying a product you can save a life. This gets everyone involved, not just the United Nations or governments around the world, it gets you and I involved. We're involved not just in a good cause or a nonprofit organization, we are involved in big, huge, life saving, world saving projects. How's that for Bono's lesson on Unselfish Self Promotion? How's that for a matrix?

This T-shirt buying, world saving Alpha Matrix goes even further than Bono and Bobby Shriver. It taps into many other Alpha Matrixes, like mine, influencing not just all of my friends and family but my readers. My wife got the red bug also. She not only buys Red products as birthday and Christmas gifts for friends and family, in many cases she tells them that if they're going to get something for her, she prefers Red products. How's that for a Matrix?

This Red Matrix is one of the most unselfish pieces of self promotion, right? Well yes, although it also taps into business, entrepreneurship, wholesale distribution, public relations, and more. You see, in order for this Unselfish Promotion to work you have to make it worth while to different people, not just for the Africans dying of AIDS. What do I mean? Well, you can buy Red products at Armani stores, at the Gap, Apple Stores, Converse and other retail stores, and yes, many people make money from this effort including freight companies, retailers, the government (taxes) and others that I can't even think of. Is this bad? Are these people taking advantage of Bono's good faith and Unselfish Self Promotion? Absolutely not. Bono understands as an entrepreneur himself that when people have something to gain they will be more interested, more into it and more committed, after all, this is what Unselfish Self Promotion is all about; looking at things from the other person's point of view. Yes, other people will profit from the Red campaign, more sales will be made, but ultimately, the goal is accomplished, to help eliminate AIDS in Africa.

This example has many lessons on promotions, on entrepreneurship, on Alpha Matrixes. It also teaches us that you can mix business with unselfish self promotion, you can mix a good cause with charity, you can mix sales and marketing with saving the world. So consider adding a touch of "saving the world" into all your Unselfish Self Promotion and I'm sure the world will pay you back!

ACT III

Advanced Self Promotion Strategies

Let's get ready to stage your real world marketing, promotion and sales of yourself. ACT III is dedicated to exploring advanced applicable techniques of how to supercharge your self promotion. We already explored in Chapter One what Unselfish Self Promotion really is, how it works as well as why it works and how I discovered it. In ACT II we learned how to apply Unselfish Self Promotions to everyday life and how to keep learning and understanding self promoting in ourselves and in others long after we finish the book. Now it's time to get out the toolbox of promotional tools, to get to the fundamentals and transform yourself into the brand manager that you need to be.

You see, now that you understand the philosophy, strategy and big picture of the Unselfish Self Promoter, now that you have pledged to become one and follow the rules of self promotion, you can now apply real world marketing and promotional strategies to promote yourself.

You will notice that we did not start the book with this chapter, we did not start by showing you internet marketing, or public relations, or image management. We did not start with any of that because if you apply these techniques without knowing how to be an Unselfish Self Promoter they will not work. Yes, you will get some success at first because they are proven marketing strategies, but your results will linger and fail. They will fail because you are not applying the "Unselfish" part of the equation to your self-promotion and it does not work like that!

These techniques will supercharge your self promotion no matter where you are or who you are; you could be in business or not, a housewife or a CEO, a nonprofit visionary or a university student, a salesperson or none of the above. Many of these tools will transcend your current occupation or job, your social standing and where you are now in your life. The tools can be applied and kept throughout your life regardless of what you are doing or where you are working. This is the point, you are not your occupation, you are not your job, and these tools keep up with who you are right now and they will adapt to who you are in the future.

You will use Advanced Promotional Tools from your Toolbox in Act III that will help you supercharge your new found promotional superpowers.

New Advanced Promotional Tools

- Internet Marketing
- Articles
- Social Networking
- Public Speaking
- Business Cards
- Marketing Collateral
- Writing Books
- Press Releases
- Your Image
- Presentation Cards

Internet Marketing

It's more than just having a Website

The internet is the great equalizer. It is a place everyone from around the world can find you if they have access to the internet. You can communicate with businesses, individuals or anyone else. You can share information, collaborate, send photos, brochures, articles and even videos.

Most people understand the power of the internet but they don't really understand what it can do for them. Here you will learn what the internet can do for you and how to exploit it and its potential.

The internet is larger and greater than you can imagine. It is a place to communicate, collaborate and commercialize. I call this the internet's three C's.

**The Internet's three C's:
Communicate, Collaborate and Commercialize**

If you want to expand your Internet Marketing Potential and Promotion visit www.MarketingMarbles.com and sign up to receive the free newsletter. It is a company I helped start dedicated to Internet Marketing.

The internet is more than just websites and your potential for exploiting the internet for promotion purposes is not limited to your business or personal websites. You can write and publish articles for thousands of readers, you can send out free or very inexpensive press releases, write electronic books (eBooks) on your favorite subject, record audios and share them, shoot photos and videos of yourself, your services, products or ideas and make them available to hundreds, thousands even millions of people. Now, how much does all of this cost? Nothing, you can do every one of these strategies for free.

The one thing that will most likely not work is building a self indulgent website and hoping to get thousands of visitors just because you claim to have the best product or the best service, the best tasting energy drink, the best price, or package or the best fabrics. You get the point. Having the "best" of anything is not a unique selling proposition. Everyone claims to have the best; this is because it's the easy way to promote. It's not creative, you just claim it and you're done.

I work a lot with consumer goods, especially with beverages. About 300 companies or individuals contact me per month just on the subject of beverages and the one thing they all have in common is that they claim to have the best taste. The second most common characteristic is that they have the best package. The third most common attribute is they have the best name. Why are they all doing the same thing? Because it's the simplest thing to do. I'm still waiting for someone to call me with the best distribution, or the best merchandising, or drop shipping sales program. Now that would really impress me.

Let's not build a "self indulgent, look at me" website. Let's say this is our First Rule in Internet Marketing.

Internet Marketing Rule #1
Don't build a self indulgent website.

I agree you have to reveal to people who you are, what you do, convey details about your business (if you have a business) or about your services, products, ideas, nonprofit organizations, etc. Yes, it is important to get your voice heard, your message across, and there are many ways to do it. The main problem is, if you don't have any visitors or traffic coming to your website how will you get your message across? You will not, you will have the best looking website and you will look at it every single day, but you'll be the only one looking at it.

One of my marketing consulting customers had just this problem. He invested about $40,000 in a decent looking website (in my opinion paid way too much). It was his pride and joy. He worked countless hours every day updating the website, making sure every word was perfect, making sure every color, photo and video was just right. He added animation, flash, photos of his product, everything. He showed everyone that walked into his office his website and wanted them to spend about 15 minutes going over the website tour while in his office. He was very proud of his work. Unfortunately, the people that walked into his office were the only ones visiting the website. Why is this? Simple, self indulgent websites don't get traffic. He was getting about 20 visitors per month. That's bad even for a poorly marked website.

Why does this happen? Why does a good looking website not attract visitors and customers? The internet is not set up that way. The internet is content based. In other words, information rules, content is king, value is the traffic magnet. Yes, we will open our old Promotions Toolbox and dig up another tool, Value.

Traffic Magnet

You will notice we have not talked about your website yet. We have not talked about how to build it, what to include, how it will look and the design. Yes, we will cover some of that in the next few pages but for now we will focus on more important things, like getting people to your website no matter how it looks.

So what attracts traffic? What's the trick to getting many visitors? Simple, there is a secret, but there is not a trick. Tricks try to do just that, trick people and search engines into getting traffic. That's no good. They only work for a limited time while the search engines learn the trick and adjust to it, they will then penalize you for using tricks. When you trick people into visiting your website they will go in, and go out after they realize you tricked them and do not have helpful information.

The thing you need in order to rank high in search engines, get links, traffic, leads, and have a killer marketing strategy is Value. I don't mean a good price, or value for the money, or value added sales. I just mean value; value before selling, value before pitching products, services and ideas. Just value.

Internet Marketing Rule #2 – Build Value

Let's look at how the internet works in terms of traffic. Let's take it from step one. People hit the internet looking for information, for entertainment, to shop, to do business and other activities. They rarely go in looking specifically for you or your company.

Knowing this, you have to provide what people look for, information, entertainment, collaboration or commerce. The same basic rules of unselfish self promotion apply to the internet. Actually, the same basic rules apply even more on the internet. They apply more because it's faster and it's bigger. What do I mean? It is faster because people are looking for information pressed for time. They don't have all day. Internet assumes speed and people go in and out of web pages quickly if they don't see what they want in as few as 3 seconds. You would do the same. Imagine if you do a search for "internet marketing" and see thousands of search results. You are looking to find the basics of internet marketing and all you see is people selling services, no information. You would go in and out of pages faster than a speeding bullet.

The internet is also bigger. You are not interacting with each visitor one on one. You are not answering the phone or even receiving emails from every single visitor. You might get 500 visitors per month, or you might get 5,000 visitors, you might even get 20,000 or 50,000. That's a lot of visitors. You could not interact with each one. This is why the internet is bigger. It's open to more people; more people can find you and receive your tailored message than from you alone.

Follow the same basic rules of unselfish self promotion to your internet strategy and to build your personal, political, business, or any other website. You must see things from your visitor's point of view. Build the website for them, to fill their needs and wants, and give them the information they are looking for.

Internet Value Example

I've done work with the beverage industry for several years now. It's very hot at the moment and growing at up to 50% per year in the "New Age Beverage" category. Companies are selling for billions of dollars and valuations are very high. Companies want to launch a new Energy Drink, a Vitamin Infused Water or other products. I did a lot of internet marketing to attract people in the industry or trying to break into the industry. I have a company specializing in beverages called Liquid Brands Management, Inc. The idea was to attract potential joint ventures to work on beverage projects.

Instead of creating a "self indulgent site" just talking about us, our company, our capabilities I created a series of websites each one with specific information about one segment of the beverage industry, all after doing research on what people looked for on the internet. So I created one website with free information about starting your energy drink, another website with free information about getting distributors, yet another site with free information on exporting beverages to Mexico, another with info on how to sell to retailers, you get the point.

What happened? I got thousands of requests for information, consulting, for business ventures and for partnerships. We got many more than what we ever imagined and many more than we could even handle. We ended up writing a book on the subject ("Build Your Beverage Empire") because we could not get back to people and answer all their questions. Yes, we offered a lot of free information, but not all information, you still need to reserve a little bit for marketing purposes, for establishing a relationship and to give more value. Following up with more information that is actually on your website is probably the most important thing in your entire internet strategy. We'll go over it in detail in our next chapters.

Building your Traffic Magnet

Remember, when you build websites with useful information and content people will find you, the internet search engines will love you and place your websites high in searches and slowly but surely you will have a solid internet self promotional machine. Your website will be a traffic magnet.

How much content or information do you need? How long will it take? These are the very questions you should be asking. You need as much information as possible. Don't think of it as a goal you will finish, you will not, it's like saying you'll finish your marketing and never do anything else again. How long will it take? It will depend on your content and on your links. I'll clarify more in the next paragraphs.

From Zero to Traffic Magnet

It takes a bit of time to start attracting traffic to your website. You need great content and lots of it, you also need people to recognize you have good content and link to your site, and you need the search engines to visit your website and see your great content and the value to their searchers. This is the perfect combination to building a Traffic Magnet.

When it comes to building content you need to provide relevant, non self-indulgent information for your visitors. This means you don't have a sales letter; you don't have just product information. You have "real information." This could be in the form of articles, case studies, how-to guides, research or other information. Remember this rule of thumb: If you're selling in your content, it's not a traffic magnet type of content. You may not think it, but this is some of the greatest promotion you'll be doing. You'll see why soon and it will all click when you learn to capture visitors' information, keep sending information and then convert them to customers, donors, voters or whatever else you're promoting.

Build new and exciting information for your website, update it and add more often. Start a blog, add videos, photos, audio and use every means of media available to provide more value to your visitors. The more information you have in different variations like audio, video and photos the more traffic you will get. The search engines will take notice and reward you for it. You see, search engines want to provide the best relevant information and content to their readers. This is what made Google great and Yahoo before it. They had the ability to provide internet searchers with the most relevant information to their particular search. When you are providing great information you are partnering up with the search engines, making their lives easier and for that they will send tons of visitors and traffic your way.

Now that we have a basic view of why you need value and how to build traffic with value we need to take advantage of that traffic. You see, just because people visit your website does not mean they will like you; they will buy from you or believe your message. What to do? There is a strategy for this as well. The strategy of getting extreme promotion from your traffic will be covered in your Internet Core Strategy.

Internet Core Strategy
Getting Extreme Promotion from your Internet Marketing

We already talked about what people look for when surfing the internet, they look for value, information and entertainment. As a promoter you look for the Internet's three C's: Collaboration, Communication and Commercialization. In this section we'll go over how to build your internet website and core strategy. All of the other strategies will be around these core techniques.

Your Core Strategy includes the three basic things you need to create a super charged internet strategy. These are: Your Websites, Your Mailing List and Content.

Yes, there are other strategies to attract people to your website but it makes absolutely no sense to attract them if you're not prepared to capitalize. It's like throwing marketing money in the trash. You have to prepare yourself for the traffic, for the leads, for the questions, for the search engines. Your Internet Core Strategy helps you prepare for all of this.

Remember your Core Strategy will start with your Content, Website and Mailing List.

Website or Websites

I say websites because a good promoter has more than one website. You definitely need to have several of them if you are a businessperson or service oriented provider like a doctor, lawyer, broker, plumber, etc. or have a serious hobby or even side business. You also need several websites if you plan on writing a book, inventing and launching a product, or are a salesperson. The website or websites that you'll have will be very basic. You don't need several high profiles, flashy sites. Instead you need sites with value.

Why do you need several website? Because you can! Imagine if you're in the retail business and you could open several retail stores in any city in the world paying only a few dollars rent or no rent, and with little or no investment in the store. How many stores would you open? One store, two stores? You would probably open as many stores as humanly possible as fast as you could. You would have large stores, small stores, fancy stores, stores with one product, stores with many products, stores in New York, London, Paris, Rome, Los Angeles, Berlin, Hong Kong and more, right? Let's apply the same premise to your websites. Rent is almost free. You can pay as little as $5 per month for the hosting. To open them is inexpensive, you can do it yourself with easy to use software I can recommend or pay someone around $100 for a simple website. Yes, I said $100. I'm not talking about super duper websites with 10 pages. I'm talking simple websites with one or two pages for starters. These types of pages are widely used by all types of promoters including fortune 100 enterprises.

If you are an executive or owner of a company you can afford to pay someone to create your websites. Maybe you even have a webmaster or a whole team. Teach them promotional techniques or send them to www.MarketingMarbles.com to learn more about online marketing. Just because they are webmasters or programmers does not mean they are marketers. If you don't have staff members I highly recommend that you learn how to use some basic internet tools. If you can use Microsoft Word you can create a website. I've done more than 50 websites on my own without knowing any HTML or other programming skills. It's imperative that you learn to do this to create your own websites and update them regularly. As the worst case scenario you can work on a blog and build your content in a blog. To get all these tools just visit www.MarketingMarbles.com and sign up, it's free.

Let's go back one step and see why we need several websites. We need them because they will bring us more traffic, they are very inexpensive, and each website can focus on one of your strengths, or products, or ideas or hobbies, books or articles. You can link each website with one another to pass around your traffic and search engines see each of your sites as an individual and different website, giving each of your websites equal amounts of attention.

Google-Yourself

Have you ever Googled someone? Have you ever Googled yourself? Did you find yourself? How many links or mentions appear with your name? You should have thousands of them. You have to make sure when someone Googles you they find you, and they find high-quality information. Ideally they will find press releases, articles and websites about you. This will give you credibility and importance.

Your Main Website

Yes, you need several websites but you also need your main website. This is the website with your name. Mine, as you can imagine, is www.JorgeOlson.com. My website is also a blog, visit it and sign up for my free newsletter packed with free self promotion information. Make sure that you own your name as a domain name. If it's already taken buy it with your middle initial, or with your nickname, or initials, or any combination. If you have a business you'll also have your main business websites and other websites around it. Now, if you have a business it does not mean you don't need your own website. Remember, this is the Unselfish Guide to Self Promotion, not to Business Promotion. Before you sell your business you need to sell yourself.

Make sure your Website has some information about you, your activities, hobbies, businesses, nonprofits, articles, about your travels or whatever you want to promote. You can have a page dedicated to business, another to family or travel, it all depends on you. Make sure you have value in your website. Free articles, case studies, photos, opinions, it has to be informative, it has to be of value with no strings attached. Write a blog or two or three, they always help increase the value factor of your website.

Don't get too fancy with your main personal website. These are the pages you might want to have:

-**Home:** General landing page with an overview of your company and products
-**Projects:** the businesses you are involved with, boards of directors you sit on, investments you have or your job, any nonprofits, politics, hobbies, or other projects
-**Products or Services:** If you are involved in business and have products or services or books or anything you want to promote you can list them here
-**Blogs:** List your blogs here or list your blog in this link
-**About Me:** Here you can place your biography. Include a few paragraphs about you and who you are. Make it interesting. List your struggles and your views not just job history or photos of your dog. You could also place your resume here when it comes time to look for a job.
-**Contact:** Here you can have your phone number, maybe mailing address (not of your home), email or a small form people can fill out to contact you.

Your email account

Let me spend a paragraph or two on the very important point of your email account. You need an email, and by this I don't mean any email, I don't mean an AOL, Yahoo, Hotmail or Google email, I mean your own email. You need your own business or personal email with your own name, this is your real name or your made up name.

I have nothing against the free email accounts. I have several of them myself and use them as a backup email and to store documents and information. You should know that they use their free emails as a form of viral marketing. As a matter of fact, a large viral marketing case study is Hotmail and how they managed to issue millions of free emails bringing visitors and visibility to their company. Hotmail was one of the first free emails available on the Internet. It was made widely available to the public in 1996, managed to get more than 8 million subscribers and sold to Microsoft a year later for $400 million dollars. Not bad for a year's work! My point is they managed to make their website and company popular thanks to you and me who used their email and sent their email to other people who learned about the company and signed in as well, creating a powerful viral marketing campaign.

We're promoting Google, Microsoft and Yahoo by using their free emails as well. Instead let's promote ourselves and our companies, products and ideas by using our own emails with our own websites. So buy your domain name and set up your email, domains are about $10 per year and they are some of the best promotional tools around. Some of the domain companies even give you a small website for free when you register with them. Go to www.MarketingMarbles.com to see your options on the best domain name companies and hosting accounts. I'll do some research for you and give you the best options possible with all the benefits and features for each one, just sign up to the free newsletter.

Internet Mailing List

Your mailing list is a part of your Core Internet Strategy. It is the most unseen part and yet it will be the most important part. Your mailing list is the collection of information that you receive from your visitors. The most basic information you will collect from your traffic is name and email. You can collect more information in other parts of your website as needed.

Picture this, you have great content, the search engines notice your great valuable information and rank you high in their searches, you start getting 200, 2000, 20000 visitors per month or more. You know you're getting all this traffic, now the real question is, what are you doing with it? Are you just trying to sell something on your website? Remember, that's not the unselfish self-promotion way. You need to take advantage of all your efforts and collect information from your visitors. Your "real" promotion is not from your website, your information, your value, the promotion really starts once you collect information from visitors.

Imagine getting all that traffic to your website and not capitalizing on it. All that effort, all that money and time is wasted. No, it's not enough to put a phone number and email on your website, you need more. You need a very simple email sign up form. This email sign up form is just a place where people can leave their name and email to receive more information on you, your information, your value.

This is how an email newsletter sign-up works from the visitors' point of view. You go online looking for information using search engines; let's say on "Travel Tips & Discounts." I'm not talking about where to buy travel websites or hotel websites, not sites selling travel, actual information on how to get great deals, where to go, how to find great inexpensive hotels and more. You find a website filled with information on the subject, stories, and photos, names of other websites, hotels and more. You are excited, you like the value the websites give and you see a place where you can leave your name and email. An email newsletter that says: "subscribe now for free to receive the latest and greatest travel tips as I discover them." You subscribe and start receiving good information from this website and this person. This is exactly what the email newsletter does. The information you send afterwards is a way to establish a relationship with your readers, so they can get to know you, your information, and your value. Now you have a captive audience for your platform, products, services, ideas, books or yourself. These people "opted" to subscribe because they see value in you and they will keep the subscription because you keep providing value. They will feel they know you, it's like talking with them every time you send a new email.

It is not enough to have a name and number or email on your website. You absolutely need a small form collecting name and emails from visitors. They are easy to make and keep. To learn more about the software I use to manage newsletters visit www.MarketingMarbles.com and join the free newsletter or send an email.

A sign-up form is simple to display anywhere on your website. I recommend that you have it at least in the home page if not in every page. It could look something like this.

Sign-up to our Free Newsletter to receive articles, case studies, and valuable information

Name: [   ]

Email: [   ]

I personally use a sequential auto-responder software to stay in touch with all my readers. I have about 10 different newsletters right now and this type of software helps me manage them all at the same time. An auto-responder is a type of software that sends emails to your entire database at once. People can subscribe and unsubscribe automatically. A sequential auto-responder sends pre-written emails to your database when you tell it to. That way you don't have to worry about sending emails at a particular time. You write them and place them in sequence and the software does the rest for you. For example, you might write five emails at once and input them in the software. Then you tell the software when it needs to send an email, it can be every other day or it can start sending them as soon as someone subscribes to the newsletter. All of these tools and more are listed in my Internet Marketing website found at www.MarketingMarbles.com.

Internet Marketing Rule #3 – Build a List

By now you are sold on the idea of having a list for any of your websites, but it is very important to have one for your own website as well. It is also important to communicate directly with your subscribers even if it's once per month. Yes, you could have someone else send their information, their articles and their views but we're trying to promote YOU, so you have to start promoting yourself. Take advantage of this easy to use and incredibly powerful strategy. You will see your email list grow steadily when you follow the simple rules and internet core strategy of providing value. You will see your readership grow by 10, 100, 1000, 10000 and more subscribers quickly if you have good valuable information. It will be your very own private fan club!

Your Second List – Always Keep in Touch

We already talked about how to build a list from internet visitors and people who find you through your internet promotions. This is a great strategy to build a trusting relationship with people you probably never will meet. Now, how about people you already know? People you have some kind of relationship with, at work, from school, your first job, or people you met in a meeting.

> **You meet hundreds or thousands of people over your lifetime. Do you keep in touch with all of them? Imagine if you did!**

Go back to your high school years, to your college years, to all your jobs and all your old and past friends. Go back to all your meetings, school meetings, teacher-parent meetings, job meetings, sales meetings, people you met at parties, and any other person you have met over your lifetime. How many people have you met? That's your immediate promotional circle.

Ok, so you missed the last 20 years. It's ok. You can still add hundreds of new contacts to your list every year. This list is your own private list and you will try to use email to communicate with everyone. You can use your email software like Outlook. It does not matter where you are in your life right now; it's not too late to start your list. You can start by adding everybody you meet to your new database. You can ask them if you can add them to your mailing list and send them an email once per month to keep in touch. I've never had someone say no.

Every time you meet a new person you should ask them if you can add them to your list. In business, pleasure, church, anywhere. You will see your database grow and grow some more. Please don't abuse this list, remember it's from people you know and you don't have to establish a deeper relationship, you already know them in person. You don't have to send them articles or press releases. You can send them a holiday card, or drop them an email once in a while to say hello, or inform them of a new book you have out, or that you'll be traveling to their city and you can meet them for coffee.

This list is also useful in important events, let's say you are moving to a new city and need help with schools for your kids or housing, you can ask for help. Or in the event you lose your job you could send an email asking for help finding a new one. Even better, let's say you have an opening in your company, you again ask your list if anyone is looking for a job. Make sure to always update your list, never send it from a generic email, always use your own email so people can identify you and go to your website if they want to. And always keep in touch, at least once per month.

You don't have to use just email to keep in touch; it's just that email is free and almost automatic. You can also use the phone, use faxes, and the mail. The mail is a great way to keep in touch with everyone of your personal contacts and a must for business contacts. We'll talk more about using the mail and phone as part of our promotional tools.

In the next few pages you will learn more techniques on self promotions. Many of them go hand in hand with your internet strategy because they build links, value and credibility for you and subsequently for your website. Some of my favorite internet related promotional strategies are Press Releases, Publicity and Articles. You will see why when you get to those sub-chapters.

Your Emails Tell Stories

Use emails as advertising and promotions

I hope after reading the chapter on your website you already obtained your own domain name and are sending emails under your own name, thus promoting yourself instead of gmail, yahoo or msn. If you haven't already done so, do it. It's the best $10 you can spend. We also covered email newsletter strategies in the last chapter. Now we'll cover your everyday emails, the emails you send to friends, colleagues, and strangers, for business, pleasure, or for your nonprofit organization. Think of how many emails you send per day, every day. How many emails do you send per week or per month or per year? Personally I send at least 20 emails per day 7 days a week. That adds up to 140 emails per week, 580 emails per month and 6,720 emails per year. These are direct emails that I send directly without any automated software and these do not include the newsletters I send out. If I were to include my newsletters I send more than 20,000 emails per month.

Imagine all those emails, all those people reading them, friends, family, colleagues, etc. Imagine all the information you can transmit to people in your email with email signatures, with messages or links to websites. Your emails are a great form of advertising and promotion.

After you have your own email you need to work on your email signature, a great promotional tool. Your signature can be set up in most web based software as well as PC and MAC based email software. You set it up once and it will appear automatically in all your emails.

This is a typical email and email signature:

> **Hello Alfred,**
>
> **It was great seeing you at the meeting yesterday.**
>
> **Your new product is amazing, please send me more information, specifications and any graphics or photos you might have. I will send them to some contacts I have and see if they want to distribute your products.**
>
> **Regards to your family.**

> **Hope to see you soon.**
>
> **Thanks,**
>
> **Jorge Olson**
> **Phone: (619) 852-6942**
> **Jorge@JorgeOlson.com**
>
> **www.JorgeOlson.com**
>
> **IMPORTANT: Make sure you visit my website and subscribe to my new email newsletter on Unselfish Self Promotion**

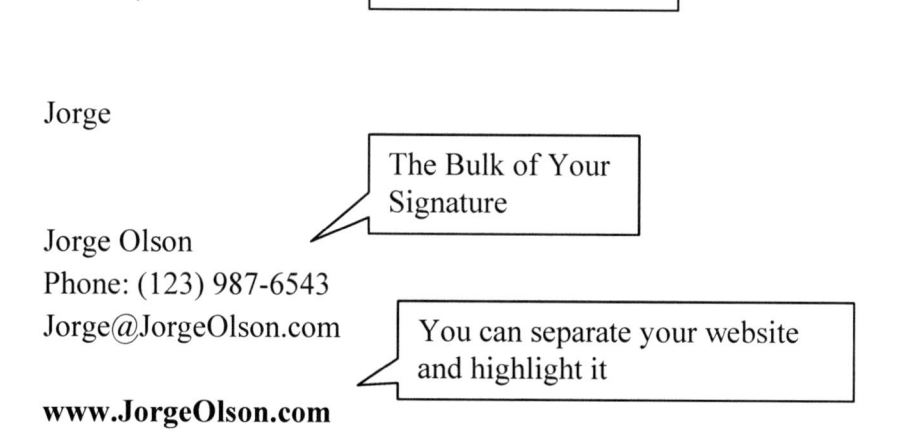

Now let's break down the signature into the different components.

-Here is the body of the email-

Thanks, — Your Signature Starts Here

Jorge

Jorge Olson — The Bulk of Your Signature
Phone: (123) 987-6543
Jorge@JorgeOlson.com

www.JorgeOlson.com — You can separate your website and highlight it

IMPORTANT: Make sure you visit my website and subscribe to my new email newsletter on Unselfish Self Promotion

> This is where you plug news, a newsletter, book or something people can take action on. Don't use branding, use unselfish self promotions. Offer a free newsletter, report or case study.

Your email is very important. You don't know how many people will see it, you don't even know how many you send per year, it could be thousands. Not to mention all the emails people forward to other people that you never learned about. This is why your email signature is very powerful as a promotional tool.

In one of my first experiments my wife was selling items on eBay and I asked her to add at the bottom of her signature "Visit our website and sign up for our wholesale products newsletter." If you have ever sold on eBay, you are aware of the amount of questions you receive from buyers about your products. My wife answered emails frequently throughout the day without realizing that the real marketing was not necessarily the leads from eBay, but the sign ups to her newsletter. The result was more than 2,000 sign ups in about 6 months. We got all these leads just from answering questions. This example can be applied to any project, product, or combined with any other tool for promotion.

Don't just use your email signature for branding, such as "Drink Coca Cola." Use it to ask for action, such as "sign up to my newsletter" or "call me for more information." Make sure your email and contact information appear automatically in all your emails so you don't have to write it over and over again. You won't believe the amount of emails I receive from people who ask me to call them and they don't include a telephone number in their signature.

Your Image Is Everything

"In Person Self Promotion"

You are with friends or colleagues at a reunion, people are seated, standing, talking, drinking wine and laughing, having fun and socializing. You walk into the room and somebody says "Wow, you have a really fine looking suit" or "That's a really nice shirt."

Does this happen to you often? If not, you will have your doubts about this chapter, but after you finish reading it you will be its champion. Let me give you my disclaimer up front. I love wearing jeans and t-shirts. As a matter of fact I take it to the next level, I live in sunny San Diego so it's sunny most of the year and I celebrate by wearing my favorite pair of "huaraches" (traditional Mexican sandals) without socks, of course, along with shorts and a t-shirt. I visit my local coffee shop and write or read or even make some calls wearing shorts and a t-shirt. I love to wear what I want to wear. It's my personality, it's my life, and it's my fashion.

You should feel comfortable with what you wear and how you look, not just with clothing but with your body. By this I don't mean you should ignore it or not pay attention. On the contrary, you should be completely aware of how you look, how you're dressed and how you feel about it. The way you communicate with others is very important in promotion, and YOU are the first thing you're communicating; the way you look, smell, dress, walk, stand, smile, speak, and interact with others. You can't promote yourself correctly if you can't promote in person. Your image is the start of "In Person Self Promotion."

The way you look is important and that includes everything about you, not just your clothes. It includes your car, house, clothes, glasses, watch, haircut, skin, I mean everything; not to mention all of your social interaction skills, posture and style.

Some people argue that these things should not matter; maybe people should have "Heart X-Ray" glasses and see what's in your heart, what kind of person you are inside. Yes, I agree, this is how it should be, and this is how we, Unselfish Self Promoters, have to see people. But the truth of the matter is this is not how it is in the real world. Not all people are like us, so we have to attract people to us, get close, so they can see who we really are. To "get close" we need a good image at all times.

Did you shine your shoes today?

I was at a business dinner one day in Houston, Texas with a Real Estate executive. He is a Vice President at a large company out of Pennsylvania and I was working as a VP of Business Development for a software company. He wore a shiny suit and a shiny tie with slicked back hair. I was about 28 years old and had already applied many of the Unselfish Self Promotion strategies so I started observing my dinner partner from across the table. He was talking about how fast he advanced within the company and how successful he was at his job. While I was paying attention to the conversation I was also observing his hands, his nails, his watch, pen, shoes, suit and tie. I could not help noticing something did not seem right. What he was saying did not match what he was wearing. Automatically I started thinking he was lying, or pulling my leg, or at least overselling.

You see, while I was listening to how skillful he was, how much he sold and grew his company I was paying close attention to his image. This was the first time I had ever met this person so I did not have anything else to go by, just that conversation and his image. He was a slick salesperson so I did not really know how much of what he was saying was true and how much was overselling or "pretending." This is why I started to scan for clues. Nowadays I do this all the time unconsciously, but back then I really used to do it without really thinking. His suit seemed like a cheap suit, his watch and pen looked fake and his shoes were not Italian. How could I tell? Well, while in college I worked at a retail store selling men's clothing including suits, shirts and ties. I was familiar with fabrics, stitching and cuts. I sold cheap suits and expensive suits, and I could tell the difference between the two.

The watch? Well, you can wear any watch you please, be it a Seiko watch or a Rolex watch, it all depends on your style and taste for watches as well as on your budget. But when you wear a fake Rolex watch you appear as if you want to portray something you are not. I happened to live in Western Europe for a while and had German, Swiss and other hard core watch fans that introduced me to the world of watches. I was not a watch expert by any definition, but I could spot a fake Rolex from across the table.

The pen? It just looked fake, it was supposed to be an original Mont Blanc pen. His shoes were not polished and looked neglected. In other words, something did not look right. What he was saying and what he was presenting were two different things.

What's the lesson of this story? If you want to feel like a million bucks, if you want others to see you and think of you like a million bucks, you have to look like a million bucks. I'm not saying you should go out and buy a fancy watch, or pen or custom tailored suits, but I am saying you should at least shine your shoes!

It is important that you look good at all times. That you pay attention to your clothing, car, accessories, hair, nails, hands, face, shoes, purse, briefcase, glasses, etc. The most important thing here is not to go out and spend a lot of money on your clothes, car or image. You have to be realistic and work with what you have. It is not a pretending game, it's about being presentable.

When dealing with clothing, cars, accessories, you have to stick to your budget but think about what you're doing. In other words, don't worry if you can't afford the 100% Egyptian cotton handmade shirt or blouse, but do worry if your blouse or shirt does not fit properly, is dirty, wrinkled, missing a button or does not match. Start with the easy things to clean up your image on the outside, like shining your shoes, cutting your nails, styling your hair, making sure your clothes are in style, clean, pressed and matching. Make sure your briefcase is in order, that your car is clean both from the inside and outside, and then move to more difficult image characteristics like being in shape or being the best dressed.

You are your own Brand Manager

Imagine if you had a talent agent, a publicist, personal lawyer, accountant, personal trainer, and nutritionist, cook, and image manager. You would be like a movie star and professional athlete all in one. This is the way you have to be, with yourself, because you have your best interest at heart, right? Well, now you need to act as your very own Brand Manager.

Your Brand Manager will keep you healthy, in shape, will keep your family, friends and associates happy, keep you happy, watch your image, watch what you say, write and do. So be your very own Brand Manager.

Dress for Success.
Remember, it's not about being trendy,
it's about looking good.

Let's go through some practical advice that will help you look better:
- Always wear clean clothes, dump anything that's torn.

- Polish your shoes – carry a small polisher in your briefcase, car or suitcase.

- Brush your teeth three times a day. This means you must carry a toothbrush in your purse or briefcase and use dental floss.

- Get a manicure once a month and always keep your nails clean. Make sure you carry a nail clipper in your purse or briefcase.

- Get a haircut once a month and style it daily if possible (if you are male keep your back and sides short).

- Shave every day, especially if you have a meeting (pay attention to your shave, go for look not speed. There is nothing worse than a half done shave where you have some hair sticking out. Don't forget to get rid of nose and ear hairs.

- Iron your clothes.

- Match your belt and suit. If you're wearing black shoes, put on a black belt, and brown shoes demand a brown belt.

- Pay attention to your shoes. Buy quality shoes that look smart and stylish. Remember, people check out shoes. Potential employers often will look at them to judge your attention to detail.

- Spend your money on shoes, not shirts and pants.

- Match your socks to your shoes or at least make sure they are a nice "bridge" from the shoes to the pants.

- Wear clothes that fit properly.

- If you wear glasses, remember they're a window into who you are. Update them at least every other year and consider style when choosing them.

- If you have to wear cologne, tone it down. Just spray a small amount into the air and walk through it. Less is more.

- No socks with sandals. And if you do wear open-toed sandals, keep your feet groomed.

- Always have a clean car, inside and out.

- Get in shape. You don't want to be seen as the heavy guy or the fat man when people point to you. It's better to be referred to as the fit guy or even the hunk!

- You can't reverse age and you don't have a lot of control over your hair loss or those small wrinkles in your eyes. However, you can do lots for your body. You can be slim and fit and even muscular. It will help your posture, your appearance and how people perceive you.

Business Presentation Cards

Business Cards or Presentation Cards?

The very first thing I would like to cover here is the meaning of the title. Cards should not only be business cards, they should also be presentation cards. Why is it? You don't have to be in business to have one. Everyone should have a "presentation card."

So what exactly is a Business or Presentation Card? What exactly is the difference?

A business card is used for business or for a job, while a presentation card is used as a personal card, it's not about your job, your career or your business, it's about you. Always remember, we're promoting YOU.

I came about this simple but very important discovery by accident while preparing to write about marketing strategies around business cards. The theme was how to create business cards, how to hand them out, and how to attract sales. When I was all set to start writing I stopped and thought for a moment about the name "business cards." It just did not sound right. Why business cards?

Thinking about it I knew why it did not sound right. It was because in my native language, Spanish, they are not called business cards, they are called Presentation Cards (*Tarjetas de Presentación* in Spanish). I started analyzing the differences in the name and in the meaning. I thought this would be a great promotional strategy for anyone, not just for people in business. Think about people with jobs who hand out their business card, what happens if they change jobs, emails or phone numbers? They can no longer be located or reached. What if you have a side business or you just want to give someone your email or website? That's when it occurred to me that we all need "Presentation Cards."

My first clue into the Presentation Cards was the language difference, but I had two more clues staring me in the face. The second clue was tradition and history. You see, in Europe it was of noble tradition to show your presentation card when announcing yourself at a residence. For example, when you knocked on a door looking for someone, let's say the man or lady of the house, you would send your presentation card with the servant or butler announcing yourself. Imagine the butler taking your card in a silver platter to the noblemen sitting by the fire in the living room. This was my second clue, presentation cards have been around for more time than I thought.

The third clue was my own childhood. You see, my grandmother had a print-shop while I was growing up. She printed her own presentation cards. My mother had some as well, and yes, I had my very own presentation cards. I was only seven years old, but whenever I met someone for the first time I would hand over my presentation card. It only had my name, my full name, *Jorge Salvador Olson Sandoval*, but I had one. At that age I did not know any better, I thought everyone had a presentation card. How else would you remember all those names from all those new people you had just met? Now it makes complete sense, although the premise is the same, how can you remember all those names from all those people? How will they remember your name? No problem, if they forget they'll just look at your presentation card.

Create Your Presentation Card

What should you have on your presentation card? For starters you should have your name. Even if you just have your name and your name alone you have a presentation card. Even if you don't add phone, email, fax, website, address, subsidiaries, cell phone, title, education, Skype, Nextel, instant messenger, you can still have a good presentation card.

Your presentation card can be simple, the most important information is:
- Your Name
- Phone Number
- Email
- Website

In this day and age just with your own website people can find you. In your website you should have all other pertinent information like address, fax, products, logos, etc. Your presentation card does not need your business name, title, logos, or other information. After all, that would be on your business card. Your website can also have all of your job information. Your presentation card is not pushy, not a hard seller, not intrusive. It promotes you and you alone, not your job, your business, trade, or products. You have to sell yourself first and then you'll sell your ideas, products and services.

Jorge S. Olson

619-852-6942

jorge@jorgeolson.com

What to do with your card

Now you have your presentation card. What do you do with it? Easy, you give it to everyone you know, meet, and have met. You can mail it to people, give it to people you meet, to your friends and colleagues, to everyone.

You can give your card to everyone because it's non intrusive, it's "politically correct." You can give it to your boss, colleagues, friends, partners, family, everyone. They will not think you are pushing a product or service to them, they will just see it as your contact information.

If you have someone interested in your products, business or services you also give them a presentation card or two. If a friend of yours has a friend that could be interested in something you do you give them two cards. Now they can contact you for business, socially, for hobbies, nonprofit or anything else.

Why don't you place your whole business information, logo and products on your presentation card? Because you are not your business, you are not your job; you are more, much more. Your card is more than your business or job. Your card can be used for all your activities and that's why it has the most important thing that you can communicate to them: your name, and secondly, a way to contact you or learn more about you.

Always have cards with you. Carry some in your wallet or purse, in your briefcase and luggage, in your car, office, everywhere. Presentation Cards are inexpensive and effective. A clean, clear card with your name and basic information is a good impression for people you meet for any reason, not just for business.

Are Business Cards Bad?

Am I saying that business cards are bad? Oh no, on the contrary, they are great. You should have them as well, especially for your business or job. They serve a purpose; they tell people what you are doing and provide more information. They promote your business or activity.

You might even have a couple of different business cards for different business. Sometimes people or prospects want to see your logo, your look and feel or your business address. For these reasons business cards are also very important.

Voice Mail From Hell

Make it Easy for People to Find You

Voice mail might sound like a simple tool used anywhere from cell phones to businesses to home phones. The reality is that the front end of the technology is very simple, the part that we all use when leaving or checking voice mail, but the backend is very complicated. These are things like programs, the computer servers or hardware. There are a lot of features, a lot of gadgets and many things you can do now to be reachable; things like having one phone number that tracks you in your office or cell phone or home phone, digital receptionists, PBX's and more. Yes, we can take advantage of all this technology to enhance our lives and our business in many ways but now we'll concentrate on the simplest forms of using voice mail. We'll concentrate on how to leave a voice mail and how to record your voice mail to get calls returned and make it easy for people to leave voice mails for you.

Have you ever called a business to inquire about a product or a service, or to actually buy something, only to be greeted by a very sophisticated voice mail system with too many options where you can't even talk to anyone to give them your money or to leave a voice mail? You can't even leave a voice mail in the sales department because you have to know the extension number to leave a voice mail. You get the old but very popular voice mail: "Using your touchtone numbers dial the last name of the person you want to reach." The problem is you don't know anyone! So you ask for a list, but you erroneously leave a voice mail for the accountant and never get a call back. You are frustrated at their phone system, they in turn most likely lost your business, and on top of it they paid big bucks for a sophisticated phone system that doesn't meet your needs.

Don't think "voice mails from hell" only happen to small businesses. Oh my! I have stories, a lot of stories, and I'm sure you have stories as well; stories of calling the phone company or the insurance company. One story that comes to mind was a time I was out of town traveling on a cruise in the Mexican Riviera. I had made a few purchases and suddenly my credit card was placed on hold and I could not use it. I dialed the "toll free number" on the back of the card but I couldn't get through because the number does not work when calling internationally. I then tried calling the operator to make a collect call but they could not get through. After a few hours of trying to get to the right department (I had a business credit card) and the right person all I got was voice mail after voice mail. Nobody could help or even return my call. Frustrating at best, especially while traveling internationally and hoping for resolution before arriving at the port, we weren't able to resolve the issue until the following "business" day.

This is a good example of just how a very small decision, like not having a direct number to the right person, can create a really big problem. It would be easy to call the number, leave a voice mail and get a call back. I have many stories just like this one but you get the idea, you can get more examples from your experiences to draw upon.

Yes, the best thing is to always get a person on the line in any situation, whether you are calling a family member or a business. The same applies on the flip side. If someone is looking for you the very best thing is that they reach you and get you on the phone every single time. But that's just not real life. You have to eat, you have to sleep, and most likely you are on the other line during the day. This is why voice mail was invented in the first place. It was not invented to make our lives harder, it was invented to make it easier, it's just that many times we don't apply technology the way we should. It's not voice mail's fault!

What we can do is make it easier for others to find us, return our calls and leave messages for us. We can't promote ourselves if people can't get a hold of us!

Receiving Voice Mails

First I'd like to talk about receiving voice mails. This includes in your home, business, cell phone or any other phone that you have. The first thing is to make sure that you actually have a voice mail. You don't want people calling any of your phones where it rings five or ten times and then stops with nothing to follow; no voice mail, no message at all. The caller will be confused and will not know if it's a real number, or if it's your number, or what happened. The expectation is to get a message after the ring, so you need to set up your voice mail, preferably with your own voice.

The second step is to have a personal voice mail, especially on your "public phones", that is phone numbers you give out. If you don't want to do it for your personal home phone that's fine, your family and closest friends will know it's your phone anyway. I'm talking about phone numbers you give out to colleagues, business associates, customers, investors or others. This would probably be your business phones, home office phone and cell phone.

This will be much easier than you think. For your voice mail just record a short, concise message with your own voice, not your assistant or your spouse, after all we're promoting you not them. Record your voice mail telling people your name and asking them to leave a voice mail. That's it! Keep it simple and keep it short. Don't make them listen to a long confusing voice mail before they can leave their voice message. Think of them, don't think of yourself. Please don't say "I'm away from my desk or on the other line;" it's obvious that you're away! Don't ask them to speak clearly and leave a phone number, if they don't want to leave it they won't. Respect their time and their intelligence. Don't coach them on how to leave you a voice mail, if they don't know how you can tell them when you return their call, don't coach on your voice mail as you will alienate many people. If you are an employee of a company or an executive or owner of a business for your office voice mail tell the caller your name and business name, if it's your cell phone or home office or you have several business just state your name, remember, we want people to recognize you, not your job, not your business, just you.

One big tip for cell phone voice mails: make sure your callers don't get the phone companies voice mail or message, make sure they just get your message. You see, if someone calls you and gets your concise voice mail where they can leave their information quickly and then get a ten second message from your cell phone company it will make it really annoying, especially if they call often and have to leave several voice mails. I am talking about the automated message that comes up after you finish leaving your voice message. This feature is easy to remove from your phone and your callers will appreciate it, especially if they call often. You will also appreciate it when they leave their phone number so you can call them back.

Now, if you are very creative and would like to leave fun, insightful but still show voice mails by all means go ahead. The key there is you have to change them weekly as people call you again you don't want them to endure the same voice mail over and over again, even if it's funny and clever. If you don't have time or you forget to change it every week stick to the simple voice mail with your name and a short recording like "You reached my cell phone, please leave a message."

Leaving Voice Mails

Leaving a voice mail is even simpler than your recording. Yes, you can be clever, funny and insightful, and you are welcome to be. Just follow this simple rule to help the other party call you back. When you call and get a voice mail leave your **full** name, your phone number and then the reason why you are calling or the action you want from them. Please ensure you leave the information in that order.

Visualize the person you called getting ten voice mails per day or more and having to listen to all of them, writing the names and phone numbers down and deciding who to call and who not to call. If you leave your phone number at the end of your voice mail they have to listen to the whole voice mail before getting to your phone number again. This is frustrating for the receiver and you're not helping in getting your called returned. So leave your phone number first, your message later. When you leave your name leave your whole name even if you are on a first name basis. Leave it even if you think they know you, or they are familiar with you. The person on the other line might get hundreds of calls, so leave your full name.

I've been working for 6 months now with a friend of mine, John, who works in mergers and acquisitions. We have been traveling frequently together, talking on the phone every week, going through many documents by email. Every time I left a voice mail I followed these simple rules until one time he told me, "Jorge, you don't have to leave your full name and phone number every time. I have you on speed dial and recognize your voice." This was my signal to stop; otherwise I would still be doing it. It's one of those "good habits" that is hard to break.
Again, I could tell you story upon story of people leaving me voice mails I never return because I could not understand them, they did not leave a name or they did not leave a phone number. Many times people that are calling to sell me something don't leave their phone number. I just don't get it! Even if you already left your phone

before, leave it again, leave it every time, make it easy for them to call you back, don't make people go and look for your phone number. Also make sure that you talk slowly and clearly, especially when leaving your phone number. I can't tell you how many calls I get with a voice mail that sounds like this: "Hello, this is Larry, remember we talked before? Call me back."

As you will see in many of my promotional strategies it all starts with common sense. You can also apply the same strategy when building your website, in your emails having your own domain and your phone number in every email, with your business cards, brochures, and with all your promotional strategies. Now that you know the philosophy and applications of Unselfish Self Promotions you are also learning the simple but powerful strategies behind your promotional toolbox.

Major Points for Leaving Voice Mails:
-Start with your full name
-Leave your phone number right after
-Leave a short compelling message
-Ask for a call back

Promotion on the Job

Get a Promotion, a Raise and buy the Company!
How to make more than you are worth

When engaged in conversation about employment, job hunting or the workplace many people complain about their job, their boss, their salary. Very often people complain they are underpaid, overworked, and their boss is not the brightest. I've never heard anyone tell me they're overpaid and they love it. You see, most times, whatever you make, even if it is a whole lot of money, you think you are worth it. You don't hear people saying I get much more money than I'm worth. Even when your friend goes to Sacks 5th Avenue to buy the expensive clothes that maybe they can't really afford they say "I deserve it." Besides, how much is too much? When are you making too much money? This has been a debate in the media for a long time in regards to how compensation packages are structured for CEO's in large public Fortune companies; especially if the company is not doing well. How much is too much? It is all relative to you, what you think, what you want and what you will do with it.

When I first got out of college I wanted to make $2,000 per month because I thought it was a lot of money and it was all I needed. Besides, I was making about $7 per hour working and surviving so it seemed like a lot of cash. At that particular moment I did not think of making $5,000 per month, or $10,000, or $100,000 per month. I did not think I could give my money away to charity or use it to build hospitals. I simply did not think I was worth it.

Lots of employees complain because they are underpaid. Being underpaid is as easy as being overpaid. Are you one of the overpaid employees? If not, would you like to be? How does this work? What is the secret to getting a raise? Well, I've been on both sides of the spectrum, earning a CEO salary before I was 30 years old and also being an employer signing paychecks. I've seen employees get 50% raises and I've seen employees being denied a $0.25 per hour raise. What's the difference? Well, unselfish self promotion, effort, and timing.

Turning unemployment into the greatest opportunity

I remember well when I finished college. I thought I would get a job in a snap. After all, I was hard working, intelligent, had great new ideas, and was willing to work very hard for anybody. Well, it wasn't easy getting a job. On the contrary, it was very hard. I wrote many resumes, interviewed literally hundreds of companies, and nothing.

Nobody wanted to give me a job. I don't quite understand why. Maybe it was because I was fresh out of college. Maybe it was because I lacked experience, I did not know. What I do know is that I should have started long before finishing college to look for a job, or at least learn how to interview, write resumes, network and look for a job.

Yes, I was searching for a job in the newspaper and internet. Not the best place to look for a job. ATTENTION job seekers: Internet job sites have one of the worst track records when it comes to getting you a job. At the same time, new job seekers think of the internet as the first way of applying for a job.

With that said, the internet can be a valuable commodity to get a job now or to network and get a job in the future. We'll talk about how to use the internet to promote you and get a job in a later chapter.

Back to the story: I really thought anybody would be lucky to have me as an employee. I thought companies would fight to hire me. I know what you are thinking, "Maybe this guy wanted a lot of cash." NO! I knew what starting salaries were. My target was to get an entry level job in the business world with entry level pay. I wanted to make $2,000 per month. To tell you the truth after a few months of looking and not finding anything I was happy with $1,500 per month.

When looking for my first out of college job I mostly searched on the internet and answered every single ad in my field. I was looking mostly under Marketing and Business. I never looked under sales. Although some of the jobs I had before college were sales jobs I did not think of them as sales jobs. For example, one of my jobs while in college was as a "clerk" at a clothing store in a local mall. It was not a great job. I made minimum wage and I was not really a clerk or a customer service rep, I was a sales guy.

I don't know if you are aware, but many of these jobs in the malls (if not all of them) keep track of everybody's sales. If you don't sell, you're out! So those so called customer service reps are sales reps. Yes, I was a sales rep. I was a great sales rep. I was number one in almost every single sales category in the store. They kept track of stats like most items sold, total sales, sales per transaction, sales per day, per month, etc.

Even though I was in sales I never considered going into sales. I always thought sales was a very hard thing to do and not very glamorous or high paying. I wanted to go into Marketing. That seemed glamorous and, after all, marketing had been one of my hobbies since I was 16 years old.

Mind you I didn't want to start as a Marketing VP or Director. I thought maybe with my great ideas and wonderful command of the subject I could start as a Marketing Manager. So I interviewed for every single marketing job out there. I mean everything.

Nop! Nothing, no job, no offers, not even many interviews. I had to take a few part time jobs to pay at least for gas. One of them was as a teacher at a language school. After all I speak Spanish and got hired on the spot. The pay was bad and I could not get more than two or three hours per day, but I needed the cash.

How I landed a job while working as a Teacher

While I was working at the language school after college in San Diego I realized most of the students that came to the language school were high level executives from companies from all around the world. I also realized most of my teacher colleagues never actually showed any real interest in their students, so they did not know where they came from, what they did, or what they wanted to do.

As a young unselfish self promoter I asked all of my students everything I could about their lives. As a matter of fact in many instances that was the topic of the language classes, to allow them to talk about familiar things in their lives, jobs, hobbies, etc. Especially in the business English classes where students wanted to learn how to conduct business in English. When asking my students what they did I realized they were hot shot executives, for example, one of my students was a Korean Stock Exchange Inspector, another was the President of Price Waterhouse Coopers, among others.

What happened? Well, I got hired by one of these executives and spurred my career becoming a CEO of a software company by age 28.

What I never understood is why my colleagues did not land high level executive positions themselves. After all they were all very smart, competitive, trusting individuals, most with more experience than me.

So how exactly did I manage to land this springboard job? I used my unselfish self promotion tools!

The best time people become Self Promoters is when they really need it, for example, when they lose their job and are looking for a new one. You send resumes, ask around, network, go to online job centers, and write letters. This is how you should be always.

Don't just look for a job, look for a boss

Be the inside person. Managers very often promote their loyal employees when they get promoted, especially in large companies. This is natural, I would do the same; maybe you would too.

Think about it. You get a promotion into another cost center, a new department or branch. You have three managers under you and another vacant management position. What to do? Well, I would suggest you start by making a list of your qualified and very trusted and loyal employees. People that like you, people you like, and people who will make you look good.

Now, on the flip side, you need to be that loyal employee as well; the one who will get promoted when the boss is promoted. If you're not that person, or you don't like your boss look for a new boss in your company or look for a new boss in a different company.

Your next boss, not your next job, will sign your promotions, bonuses, and pay checks. If you are not happy with your boss right now, change your boss! If you are at a dead-end job or will not rapidly advance in your job change it. I know it's not easy, it's comfortable to stay in one place but, your future, your health and your family are more important than comfort.

What to do? Change your boss! This can be your boss at a job, your board of directors at a business, or investors, or chairman. Whoever it is, change it. Look for someone that you like, respect, in a business that you want to be in, even if you have to change it from where you are right now. You are smart; you will learn a new industry.

Look for a company you want to be involved in as an employee, investor, executive, or in any capacity and look for a key person in the company you want as a boss and call them, email them, meet with them, don't give up until you get in front of them.

Too good to pass

There is always a good deal out there, it just depends if you are right for that deal at that moment. What do I mean? I mean opportunities are out there all the time; sometimes you are ready for them sometimes you are not. Some other times you are over them! For example, let's say you are offered a job to make $3,000 per month. Is it a good deal or a great opportunity? Careful, it's a trick question! The answer I'm looking for is "it depends." It depends on when you are offered the job and where you are at the time of the offer. Imagine if this is a good opportunity right at this point in your life, now imagine you are just out of college, is it a good opportunity? Now think you only have to work 20 hours per month to get it, is it any good? How about we're in a recession and there is 30% unemployment? Get the drift?

Good opportunities are out there, you just have to find the opportunity that you want right now. Not only that, you also have to identify the better opportunities that come when you are in a comfort zone.

Managing vs. Leading

When you lead, other people follow you because they want to follow you. When you just manage they obey because they don't have a choice. Stop managing people and strive to be a leader.

What are the key differences between just a manager and a leader? Well, the differences are vast but for our lesson we'll stick to the main differences. For example, you can place a manager in a position of power but you can't place a leader in a position of power. That power is given to the leader by their team, or the people who they lead. With a manager the power is implied. They can fire you so they have power.

In sales management leading is even more difficult. You have to get constant updates on meetings, proposals, pricing and sales. Not only that but you have to motivate employees on a daily basis. This takes effort, time, and leadership.

Leading salespeople is one of the most difficult tasks for any manager. For example, one of my clients is a high level executive that is constantly calling his sales directors and managers for status reports. He calls daily, twice, even three times per day asking "How much will you sell" or "What are you doing?" or "How was the meeting?" His employees are often irritated by this and feel micromanaged. They don't know whether to give straight answers or beat around the bush. Often they don't want to commit to any hard sales numbers and many times they just don't pick up the phone.

Yes, this person pays their salary, he's the boss, he can give them a raise, even a bonus, and yes, he can fire them. Now, this does not mean he's a leader. In this case, he's far from it.

A sure way of knowing if you are a leader is by the calls you have to make to get information. Managers make calls, leaders get calls!

Leaders get calls

What kind of executive are you? Do you want to be just a manager or a leader? Take the "phone call test." Are you constantly calling employees or colleagues or do they constantly call you? If you call them you could use a dose of leadership.

This is a quick way of identifying a leader. They get phone calls from everyone including colleagues and employees, many times from friends and family members. Leadership does not stay confined to the office!

In sales management leaders get frequent calls up to three or four times per day from salespeople telling them about how great the last meeting was or how they closed the much anticipated deal. They know their leader will always help them, mentor them, and have their best interest at heart.

Yes, leaders are mentors, but more importantly, they care deeply about others, especially their employees. Many time leaders protect their employees, they want to make them better, smarter, richer even, trying to get them more commission, an extra bonus or a raise. Leaders care about their employees' well being, about their families, their working conditions and their happiness.

Web 2.0 & Social Networking

Learn How to Self-Promote in the New Web 2.0 World

So what exactly is this Social Networking, Social Media and all of this Web 2.0? Why is it so important and how can I use it for self promotion?

First of all let's start by exploring what Web 2.0 is and how it is different from the "typical" web that you and I know, or Web 1.0. All of the other definitions like Social Networking and Social Media are part of this Web 2.0 medium so we'll bunch them all together.

About Web 1.0

Web 1.0 is the web we all know and grew up with (unless you are 12 years old, then you grew up with Web 2.0). It is a world wide web filled with informative, personal, and business information related to us in the form of websites. Nowadays there are websites for almost any type of business and every possible topic. You can find news, universal information, photos, videos, everything.

You see, in Web 1.0 you get information, news, videos and other content but you can't push back content, ideas, or information. You just have to look for websites and read them. If you have a company website you list your products, services, contact information and any other relevant content. If you have a personal website it works pretty much in the same manner. You go in, you read and then you exit the site.

In Web 1.0 you do have a little collaboration, but mostly for large companies working in intranets or extranets to publish information accessible to others in the company, or to collaborate in specific projects or documents.

The world of Web 1.0 is a great world. You can find almost anything very quickly on the internet, read, send emails, publish a website for you or your business and show it to the world.

All right, by now you may be asking yourself why we need a Web 2.0 if Web 1.0 sounds so good. It really does, but it's lacking one thing, and maybe one thing only, but it is a very large thing. It's lacking **interaction**.

About Web 2.0

The new web is founded on the one thing that's lacking from Web 1.0, and that is interaction. Web 2.0 is all about interaction. You don't just push information to your readers, customers or website visitors, you share information and they can respond to that information and even share their own information or opinion instantly.

Web 2.0 is filled with interacting blogs, video places, music websites, news sites, social networking sites, business or professional sites and more.

Interaction is the number one feature of the new Web 2.0 and it is represented in many different ways in all websites of all sizes. You as a visitor to a website can create your own profile with your photo and personal information, you can seek out and make connections with other people, you can comment on any topic, start topics or upload articles, videos or audio files.

These 2.0 websites include websites with: blogs, news, social media, social networking, videos and music.

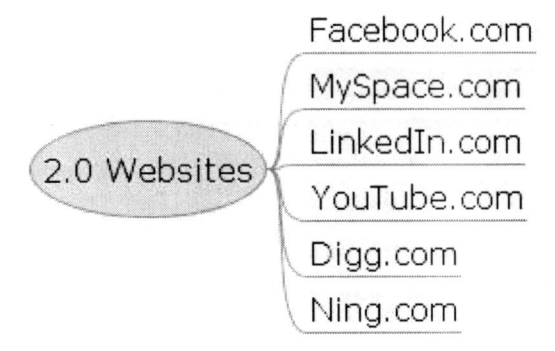

```
                    Facebook.com
                    MySpace.com
                    LinkedIn.com
    2.0 Websites
                    YouTube.com
                    Digg.com
                    Ning.com
```

Differences between Web 1.0 and Web 2.0

Many Web 2.0 websites were created specifically as Web 2.0 websites. They are made from the ground up to let you interact with others as much as you like. You are the main topic of such networks like Facebook.com and MySpace.com.

Other Web 2.0 sites like LinkedIn.com have a common topic and they let you work and interact around that topic. In the case of LinkedIn.com the topic is "professional connections." The site lets you create a profile, select your area of business, job or other professional connection and even allows you to make new connections. It has little interaction through group questions and answers but this is not the main theme of the site. The main theme is making professional connections.

Other sites are not made specifically for networking. These are the ones that let us compare the Web 1.0 and Web 2.0 world. For example, if you take a traditional news website like NBC you notice it is a Web 1.0 site. They provide information to you and you read it. In a Web 2.0 environment you would be able to upload or suggest news stories that you read somewhere else. You and others can comment on the news and even make connections with people who like the same types of stories. The most notable news and content Web 2.0 site is Digg.com.

Now let's explore personal and business websites. A traditional website has information about you or your company and products or even has information about a particular topic. It then provides that information to the readers in a one way direction. If the website is updated often and has good solid information the search engines will index it, give it good positioning in search engines and send you traffic. This is how almost all websites are currently developed and presented.

Start Modernizing Your Website

To modernize your website the name of the game is "Interaction." You have to make it more interactive and allow your visitors, friends, customers and prospects to collaborate and interact. This will not only make for a better website but it will supercharge your Unselfish Promotion. You see, when you have an interactive website people feel closer to you, they feel they know you and they can trust you. They are not just part of your customer base, now they are part of your network.

You can start your way to web modernization by adding a blog. A blog is nothing more than adding regular comments on your website and allowing feedback. I recommend WebPress.com as your free blog software. The blog is a tool that allows you to add comments about yourself, your interests, products, travels or anything you want. People find your blog if it has attention-grabbing content and actually subscribe to your blog so they can find out what you are writing about.

By now you are well versed in Unselfish Promotion. Use what you know to write your blog. If you write selfishly you will not get any visitors. If you write with the principles of helping others solve problems, entertaining or sharing valuable information you will get lots of visitors.

A blog is the easiest and most inexpensive way to start your Self Promotion using Web 2.0 in your personal, business or non-profit websites. There are also blogging communities like MyBlogLog.com by Yahoo.com that let you make connections and relationships with bloggers and people who read blogs.

Many new websites have a blog as the centerpiece of their website and list their products, services or ideas around the blog. They also link to all of their social network profiles so that if you belong to Facebook.com or LinkedIn.com you can find them there and connect with them.

You can also add tools from the Web 2.0 world like audio files or podcasts and feature videos, maybe from YouTube, to make your points. You can create and upload both video and audio files to social media websites for free and then share them in your own website. Again, if you provide good unselfish content you will see amazing results.

To really use Web 2.0 to its maximum potential you need to use Social Networking sites like Facebook.com, MySpace.com, LinkedIn.com and many others. There are also many niche Social Networking Sites about any topic that you could imagine. Start joining these social networks and become an "Open Networker" in every site. Create groups and discussions, make connections and provide content. You will start seeing results immediately.

Now, if you are really committed to Web 2.0 and already have a strong message you want to communicate you can open your own social network. There is software that you can use for free that lets you create your very own social network and invite others to join. It is your network, your topic, and you manage it. I use Ning.com for the Beverage Business social network I created called BevFan.com. It is a network around the beverage industry and helps entrepreneurs create, bottle, and market their beverages.

You can create your own social network around a topic, idea, business, hobby or product. The trick is to fill your social network with as many members as possible. Try to start with a goal of at least 100 people in your network. Invite them through your email newsletter. We talked about this strategy in past chapters.

What is an Open Networker?

If your plan is to use Social Networking as part of your unselfish promotion strategy you have to be an open networker.

What exactly is an open networker?

When you join communities online you can be a close networker or open networker. A close networker is when you don't want to connect with people you don't already know and you don't want other people to see your photo, your profile or your information. You maintain your privacy and all your information is private. The network in this case would work more like an intranet than a social network.

You are an open networker when you allow anybody and everybody to connect with you and view your information, photo, biography, and even your contacts and interests. For me this is the purpose of networking, I use it as a form of unselfish self promotion.

Make sure you upload your photo and complete your profile in each network you join. If you don't have a photo people will more likely not click on your profile. Link to your personal website or blog from your networks and make connections and friends.

Why is Social Networking important for your Unselfish Self Promotion?

You increase your contacts and connections exponentially when you become involved in social networking. You can connect with hundreds or thousands of people in a few months and even have access to their connections. You can also interact with your connections, send them information, and talk about similar interests, products, or business. If you use the same principles you learned with Unselfish Self Promotions and apply them in social networks you will have a world platform for your promotions. From your computer you can promote to hundreds of millions of people.

I see social networks as the future (near future) of all internet surfing, transactions, communications, and business. Every business will have or belong to one or several social networks, not to mention every business executive. Most are already on social networks.

Chapter Takeaway:
-Have a Blog
-Join Social Networks
-Be an Open Networker

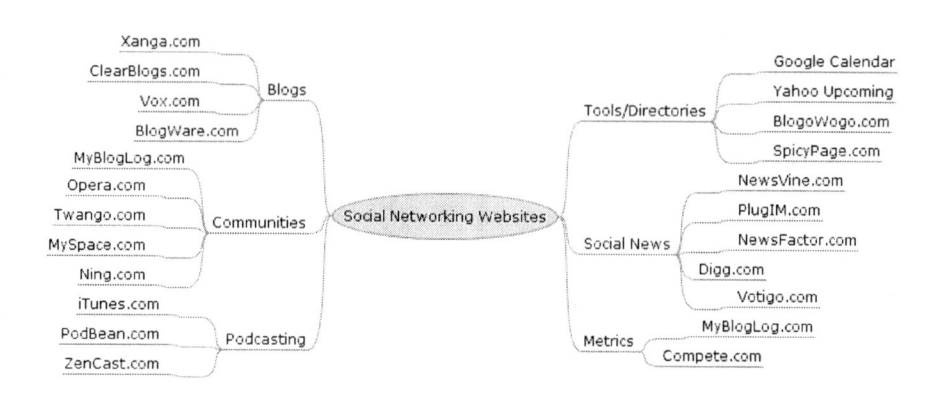

Social Networking Websites

- Blogs
  - Xanga.com
  - ClearBlogs.com
  - Vox.com
  - BlogWare.com
- Communities
  - MyBlogLog.com
  - Opera.com
  - Twango.com
  - MySpace.com
  - Ning.com
- Podcasting
  - iTunes.com
  - PodBean.com
  - ZenCast.com
- Tools/Directories
  - Google Calendar
  - Yahoo Upcoming
  - BlogoWogo.com
  - SpicyPage.com
- Social News
  - NewsVine.com
  - PlugIM.com
  - NewsFactor.com
  - Digg.com
  - Votigo.com
- Metrics
  - MyBlogLog.com
  - Compete.com

For a complete list of social networks go to www.JorgeOlson.com

Write

Want To Be Famous?
Start Writing

Writing is one of the greatest and most noble ways of unselfish self promotion. Through your writing you are able to entertain, you can teach, you allow your readers to imagine and dream. Writing is truly one of the ultimate tools for unselfish self promotion.

In addition to entertaining, teaching and evoking ideas and emotions on your readers, you are also spending time with them. You are establishing a relationship; they feel like they know you. You can write anything that comes to mind: articles, blogs, poetry, stories, fiction, and non-fiction. You will get closer to people when they spend time reading what you wrote.

Imagine if you write a book that takes a few hours to read. Your readers will know that you wrote it, they will know who you are, maybe what motivates you. Even if they don't know you personally they will feel a connection to you. After all, you've been in their house and they've spent hours with you and your thoughts.

If you think you can't write reexamine your thinking. If you can talk you certainly can write. If you don't believe me or are skeptical just record yourself having a conversation about family, politics, religion, business, your job, travel, sports or any other topic you enjoy. Just record a normal conversation where you're conveying your point of view. I bet you can talk for hours! Do it with your friends over a pot of coffee. Then play back the conversation and type it. You are now a writer!

My tip to you is to write like you talk, even with the mistakes, colloquialisms and expressions. Remember, you have to be who you write. Don't try to be YOU the person and YOU the writer. It has to be the same. You have to express yourself when you write. Remember writing is what will stay here after you are gone; things like your ideas, impressions about life, how you feel about friends and family, what you were thinking about in a particular day. Your thoughts will stay if they are on paper even after you are gone. Your unselfish self promotion will live when you don't.

Writing Ideas

Try to make an effort and include writing in your lifetime. It doesn't necessarily have to be a book, take on a blog, write notes to your kids, mother, brothers or sisters, or to your spouse. Even if it's once per month, tell them what you are thinking or why they are important and special. Would you like your loved ones to write to you every month and tell you how special you are to them?

I started a habit of writing to my godsons and goddaughters. I have many of them so it's not a two minute job. However, I don't see them every day or even every single week but I think about them constantly. They are all important to me, and I worry about their future. They don't know this yet because they are still small children, but one day they will understand and remember. They too will be grown-ups and have children or godchildren of their own and maybe they can pass on the tradition and do the same for them.

I write to them with no particular order. I keep a journal and tell them what I did that day, or that I was thinking about them, or that I did something with their parents. Some writing they will understand when they are older; some I write so they can read and understand today.

Write when you have strong feelings or emotions. Sometimes these emotions will be powerful ones and you can preserve the moment and stay in your emotional high. Sometimes you will have bad experiences and emotions. Write about those also, even if they are day to day or trivial. For example, if you had a bad experience in a store write about customer service or "what not to do" in retail. Is someone bugging you at work? Write about communication skills or how to have a perfect workplace environment. Not only will you let out some steam, maybe there is an interesting article or even an inspiring book in there somewhere.

See your writing as an X-Ray of your ideas. Bring them out. Write about what you feel, about your dreams, about the stories you tell yourself in your own mind. Write about your feelings for your family or teach people how to be better parents, better travelers or employees. Try to communicate so that people learn from you; not just from your knowledge but from your experiences and yes, even from your mistakes.

Keep a folder in your computer labeled "Writing" and have sub-folders for business, travel, sports, investing, family and any other activity, thought or interest you may have. When you have something to say open a document and start writing. Save your document under the appropriate folder. You will soon have your very own library. Now you can decide what to do with your writing. You can start a blog, publish a book, articles or send letters to your family.

Another writing tool is the good old fashioned pen and paper. Keep a journal or notebook in your briefcase, your purse, your car or somewhere you can quickly retrieve. I try to keep a hardcover journal with me at all times and when inspiration strikes, it's easy to jot down notes. Keep the notebook handy when you are reading, traveling, or waiting somewhere in line!

Teach children to read and write. I was very lucky to be born into a family of artists. They weren't very business or money savvy, but who needed that when I was exposed to literature, philosophy, painting and theater. Some form of art was always present in my everyday life. My mother encouraged me to read and write since I was a little kid. She also told me stories and had more than one thousand books in the house.

The skill of writing is closely tied to reading. The more children read the more they will understand books and get used to books. Once in a while give children diaries instead of toys and make writing an enjoyable game. They will have fun and learn one of the best skills to have in school, in life, and in unselfish self promotion.

Speaking

Communication starts with speaking
How good of a speaker are you?

Speaking is the center of communication in our world and all its cultures. All other forms of communication complement or are somehow related to speaking. The question is: How good of a speaker are you? You should be a wonderful speaker, you learned to speak at a young age and probably practice speaking every single day. You speak at home, at work, socially, in sports, on the phone, in person, to one person or to many people. Maybe you even speak more than one language!

We speak so much and so often that most of the time we don't pay attention to how we are speaking. We speak in front of one person; we speak to several people over coffee or socializing with a glass of wine. In our job or business we need to speak with everyone, sometimes you feel like a professional speaker!

Strangely enough the second best way of learning to speak better is by listening (the first way is by speaking). In a previous chapter you learned the importance of listening to people, to their thoughts, their dreams, their problems, not just their words. Now you also have to learn to listen to their words. Observe people and how they speak, how they moderate their voice, the spaces between words or sentences; start by understanding how every person speaks differently.

When you are watching the news on TV observe and analyze the newscasters, reporters or people being interviewed. Are they good speakers? Do they express themselves correctly? Do they inspire trust? Do they stumble on words or use crutch words like mm, ah, or um?

Self Promotion and Speaking

Speaking is an integral part of self promotion. You must have a goal of being the best speaker you can be and achieve it quickly. Others will judge you based on your ability to speak and communicate. Great communicators don't just speak, they inspire, they are leaders, they motivate. Be a great communicator, apply the skills of unselfish promotion and you will be unstoppable!

Almost every single time you speak you are using self promotion. People look at you, they listen, and they interpret and judge you all in a fraction of a second. That's a lot of promotion, and a lot of judging!

You are faced with multiple speaking opportunities every day. You might speak at work with employees, customers or suppliers, if you go to the doctor you speak with the receptionist, with the nurse and with the doctor. At the post office you might speak with the post office employee and maybe with one or two people while standing in line. Every time you go out you have an opportunity to practice speaking and to use your new unselfish promotion skills, like smiling.

Next time you speak pay attention to yourself. Notice your volume, your tone of voice, your expressions, posture and even your hands. Do you make eye contact? Do you modulate your voice or do you have a monotone? Are you asking questions and being engaging or just rambling on and on?

Public Speaking

Oh yes, now we get to the good stuff! Public speaking is supposed to be the number one fear among people in the USA, even more than death! I bet it's also true in other countries. Fortunately you are an unselfish self promoter and are not afraid of anything, especially of a few people listening to you. Or are you?

Public Speaking is a great self promotion tool to have and sharpen. You use your communication skills together with your unselfish self promotion and become a great speaker. To become a better public speaker use the same qualities you have when you speak without a public, when you speak with your friends or your family. The best speakers are the ones that speak to each person as if they were the only person in the audience. Forget about the many, speak to each person.

The very best public speakers are in front of hundreds, even thousands of speakers and don't seem larger than life, don't seem like rock stars or celebrities, the very best speakers can communicate with you, they can influence you, motivate you. They seem to speak or refer to you and just you. I think this is the number one quality to have as a speaker, to make each person feel they are the ones you care about; they are the ones you are talking with. It also makes it easier to you, the speaker. You don't need thousands of people to be a public speaker. You can speak to your colleagues at work, or to a group of friends, or in a wedding. Wherever you are, try to imagine you are in the middle of your living room speaking with your very best friends and closest family members. That's exactly the same style that will make you a great speaker. Speak like if you were in your living room!

Don't forget to teach your children to speak. Start them young; teach them a poem or a story or even a song. Encourage them to do a play for you and the rest of the family. Expose them to being the center of attention as in public speaking. I was lucky enough to go through that process as a child. My family taught me songs, poems, and stories that I had to perform to every person that walked into the house.

Since the age of seven I competed in recitals and monologues in front of more than 2,000 people. As I grew up and continued competing I still got nervous, but I wanted to be there! Further along I did many years of youth community service where every week you had some kind of public speaking in front of your student friends. I did not see it as public speaking then, but it was, it was great practice.

Join Toastmasters

Toastmasters is a non-profit organization created to help you better yourself as a public speaker, communicator and leader. I'm a member of Toastmasters International and you can too. It is very inexpensive to join and the benefits are enormous. You meet once per week for an hour and a half and you follow a very useful format to help you improve your public speaking. Don't worry; you don't have to speak at first. You can go to the meetings as a guest as many times as you want and see what it is all about. You will meet interesting individuals that want to help you better yourself as a speaker, communicator and leader.

You can visit their website at www.Toastmasters.org

Toastmasters have many clubs all around the world so I bet you will find two or three clubs around a 2 or 3 mile radius from where you live. When I first looked into Toastmasters I went to their website and searched for a club in San Diego, California where I live. I found five clubs near my home meeting at different days and different times so it was easy to pick the most convenient day and time that fit my schedule.

To be frank I did not pick up and immediately go to the first meeting. I procrastinated for about a month and thought about it for another two weeks. After all, it's not easy for me to just go into a meeting or room filled with strangers. No, I'm not a social butterfly as you might think. I use the same techniques as you will from this book to help me be more social and outgoing. Yes, I procrastinated for a time and finally decided to go. What I found was the best group of people you can imagine; fun, open minded, happy to see me, diverse, humorous, and very helpful. I was hooked from the first day.

I encourage you to visit your local toastmaster chapter and see for yourself what they have to offer. It is not scary, it is a lot of fun and you learn and better yourself while making new friends all at the same time.

The toastmasters meetings have a very well organized format that really impressed me. It is not just talking or speaking. You also learn to manage your time, to manage a meeting, to introduce people, and you are entertained for the entire meeting even if you don't participate on your first visit. Again, please go to your chapter meeting. You will learn a new and important unselfish self promotion skill with the help of a team.

Record Yourself

I know you may not be an expert at public speaking or a professional keynote speaker. It does not matter; it is still a good idea to record yourself speaking. Take opportunities at work or even when you join Toastmasters to record yourself speaking. It does not matter what topic you are covering, it does not matter if it's not business related, just record yourself.

Your recording is one of the best forms of unselfish self promotion you can use. After all, you are teaching something or covering something of interest in your video. Maybe it's about the economy, or about travel, or even marketing or business. It does not matter, record it, and you will be able to use it in your website, your blog, or for the future to share it with your kids or grandkids. At the very least you will be able to see the video and judge yourself all the while making any necessary adjustments and learning from your recording.

Videos can be used on your profile in Social Networks, they can be used when applying for a new job, to promote yourself for your business, your book, or any of your many life projects. When you visit my websites you will see I try to incorporate videos everywhere, in my personal blog or websites like www.JorgeOlson.com and in other businesses like my beverage consulting and incubator business at www.LiquidBrandsManagement.com. I also upload my videos of keynotes or presentations to YouTube and 30 other video sites that help with promotion and distribution of the videos. Find other examples at my keynote speaking page www.JorgeSpeaks.com and even in this book's website at www.UnselfishPromotion.com.

If you would like more information on video self promotion and marketing go to www.MarketingMarbles.com. This is a marketing & software solutions company that provides full service Social Web 2.0 marketing including video strategies for small and large businesses.

Final Thoughts

I hope you take it with you

You are the most important chapter in this book. Now, with more information, tools and power you can write your own chapter; literarily and figuratively. Since you have an open invitation to go to my website and contact me, tell me what you think about the book, or even better, tell me how you feel and how you use your newly found information in your life, your family or your business.

Yes, please tell me how you use your unselfish self promotion. How it influenced you and your plans. You can email me or use the blog at www.JorgeOlson.com to tell your stories, share your thoughts and your plans.

Writing a self promotion book with social responsibility is not the simplest project. You need to have real usable information and immediately usable tools such as the ones found in ACT III. This way you can master the self promotion world and apply and tailor the information and use it in marketing, in politics, business, or everyday life.

Yes, this is a self promotion book; it is also an "unselfish" book. The book and information within is a way to accelerate your development, growth, even wealth, so you can be happy and then help others. So in theory it is not only a self promotion, it is a world promotion book!

The trilogy of self promotion, marketing and sales, what makes a great business book are very easy to compile, write and teach. Even the most modern of business information and strategy is easy to document and express. Now, add self-improvement, motivation and social responsibility to the equation and you have Unselfish Promotion. This was my intent, to create a great business book together with an impressive self-improvement and social book. After all, society, people, economics, and business all intertwine. Why shouldn't a book do the same?

At the end of the day (and of the book) I truly wish you will find Happiness, Health and Wealth in your Unselfish Self Promotion life odyssey.

*Promote yourself to your heart's desire,
then promote others.*

Contact Jorge S. Olson

Website & Blog

www.JorgeOlson.com

Motivational Keynote Speaking

www.JorgeSpeaks.com

Breinigsville, PA USA
11 November 2010
249183BV00001B/118/P